A
SPOT
on the
FLOOR

BRENDA REYMANN

With bountiful love to my husband Larry,
my children;
Sarah and David,
and my cherished grandchildren.

And in memory to my beloved aunts,
and to the best and wisest
Godly mother, Naomi Davis.

TABLE OF CONTENTS

A Note from the Author

I, a child of eight years, along with other young cousins, were not allowed to partake of homemade chocolate-chip cookies and cherry Kool-Aid on the pretty camelback sofas or the rose-patterned armchairs that graced the living rooms of our mothers and aunts. As such, we found 'a spot on the floor,' from where we listened with eager ears to their tales of growing up on a farm in a small West Virginia town. The stories that were funny and sweet and told in noisy laughter were ones of eggs, a mule, and a brave 13-year-old, which could be shared with small fry. Whereas the stories that spoke of adultery, betrayal, murder, and revenge were shared in somber and quiet tones with the adult cousins we 'small fry' had now become— where, in deference to our aging and beloved mothers and aunts, we once again found 'a spot on the floor,' but this time with store-bought cake, cigarettes, and mugs of strong coffee.

The stories and tall tales in my book are the ones that were repeated over and often to new generations and that I remember so well.

Writing the seven short stories has been a way for me to revisit the past, with a longing to relive those days in the company of the caring, crazy funny, loving, and incredibly strong women who shaped my life and who my heart still misses beyond measure.

It is also to fulfill a dream of sharing pieces of family history with my children, for as my daughter has often said, "Mom, you really should write these down."

The people I've captured in the texture word all breathed life and are/were my relatives, with their remembrances as a basis for the telling of each tale. 'Evie,' a tiny girl fond of eggs and whom my mother Naomi, loved, Tim's wild mule ride, fiery peppers, the evilness in Reba's life, and the revenge for a horrible deed are all true. But much of the storylines that ensued are primarily of my imagination and never took place.

Most of the protagonists of the stories are long gone, but out of respect, I've changed the names to protect the innocent as well as the guilty.

I hope my stories will bring forth a good read with its parts of truth, its parts of fiction, and its enhancement of true past events to where you, too, will want to find 'a spot on the floor.'

EVIE

*"This time, like all times, is a very good one,
if we but know what to do with it"*

- Ralph Waldo Emerson

Spring 1942

Evie was as cute as that preverbal spotted puppy. Evie was four years old. Evie was poor. And Evie was hungry. To a small, improvised child, a faraway war doesn't seem any different from everyday life, especially in the mountains of West Virginia. All that mattered was that her stomach ached, and hunger was a constant companion.

Then there was Miss Naomi. And Miss Naomi shined like the brightest star in Evie's world. The first time Evie came with her mother to work for the Jacksons, it was Miss Naomi who took notice of the small, shy girl hanging on to her mother's well-worn skirt. And it was Miss Naomi who heard Evie say, in a soft and childish voice, "Evie wants an egg..."

The war had landed in Sandy Creek, West Virginia, like a load of soured hay. It stank, and it hurt.

In the corner of a paper-chinked wood cabin, on an old scarred hand-crafted table, was a small woven basket of pink and green left over from an Easter hunt at the Sunlight Baptist Church. Though the small bits of chocolate eggs and colorful jelly beans were long gone, in its place were the precious white, cream, and speckled eggs Miss Naomi had laid with care and affection. Lowering her face, Evie's eyes tenderly watched over a tiny baby boy she rocked in her arms, who Evie loved dearly but was relieved that she didn't have to share her eggs with.

She studied the cabin and, with something she would later know as pride, was glad her Mama kept the little home 'neat as a pin,' as Evie heard one woman at church comment about her mother. It made Evie feel good inside and made the void of food feel easier.

At a small, open fireplace stood Evie's father. Tall, with dark brown hair and green eyes that told of his Welsh heritage, he was a kind man with a gentle smile and calloused hands that could lovingly embrace a wee girl when she was scared of storms that would almost tumble the old cabin to the ground. What most people noticed, though Evie didn't seem to notice and didn't care, was that Daddy limped on a twisted foot and a leg that hadn't healed correctly, along with an arm that hung in a strange way by his side. Daddy was what they called a 'coal loader.'

On a normal day that began at 7 am and lasted as much as 12 hours in a five-foot-high tunnel, Daddy loaded chunks of black dust-covered rocks into a wooden sled to be dragged up and out of a big hole in the ground. But on a day that turned out to be nothing but normal, Daddy lay in a cascade of those rocks that almost crushed the life out of him and brought an end to days of work in a dark world that would bring even greater poverty to his family. The coal company doctor did the best he could and even saw that Daddy was taken to a big hospital in Charleston, but the damage was bad, and parts of Daddy's body would never be the same. The mine gave Daddy a job above ground, but the pay barely provided the basic food for a family of four, but they survived.

Momma stirred a pot of beans on a dilapidated iron stove and, using the last of a ham that was from the county welfare office, was preparing supper. Evie knew her eggs would find their place in the greasy iron skillet shortly, which made her feel a little sad, but she also knew that Miss Naomi had placed extra eggs in the pockets of Evie's small, faded, peony-flowered apron. Mamma said they were Evie's and hers alone, for Evie did love her eggs.

As instructed, Evie carried 'odds and ends' of old silverware from a small wooden chest along with pretty flowered bowls and saucers that Grandma Viola had given Evie's mother on her wedding day. The bowls were filled with beans, ham was placed on the saucers along with a sliver of cornbread, and there, next to it all, lay the most beautiful fried eggs Evie had ever seen. Heads were bowed, and thanks were given, and that night, Evie slept with the fullest belly she had had in a long time.

Evie and Mamma worked as often at the Jacksons as they could, and it turned out to be quite a lot, along with many other struggling families that lined the hollows of rural central Kanawha County. The names of Jones, Hackney, Lewis, Morris, Harper, and many others—descendants of those who had followed trails made by Indians and surveyors and settled along the Pocatalico River—regularly showed up for whatever task they could fulfill at the Jackson farm for a small amount of pay. The Jacksons were better off than most country people during a war that was filled with rations and unemployment.

Dr. Alden Jackson, DVM, was a veterinarian who traveled the 'hills & hollows' of the many forks of the Little Sandy Creek and the Pocatalico River in a well-used 1939 Chevrolet pickup or many times on horseback when the truck was low on gas, to treat animals small and large. In freezing rain or summer heat, Doc Alden Jackson attended his patients with the care and dignity he learned from his father, Dr. Grant Jackson, MD, a beloved country medical doctor, who also traversed the mountains on horseback to places where his 1936 Plymouth sedan wouldn't go. Owning 200 acres of rolling hills, flat mountain fields, and clear-water creeks, Alden Jackson raised cattle, swine, sheep, and the wonderful chickens that provided Evie with her glorious eggs.

Every day at the Jackson's was a day of hope for Evie because Miss Naomi had come to adore the wee girl. She saw Evie as a small copy of herself—straw-colored hair, hazel eyes, with a brown nugget center, and a small smile that took over her face when it appeared. At the end of the day, Momma would find her basket with little chunks of cheese, maybe a small jar of peach jam, or a few round potatoes, or teabags, and a tiny amount of rare sugar that had been sneaked in while Momma and others were working. And for Evie, the day always brought lovely eggs that were gently carried home in the pink and green basket.

The summer of '42, to a child of four years, seemed to pass with great speed of long hot days of helping Momma and Daddy or playing with the baby boy named George and nights of child-size ponderings. Evie loved the time at the Jacksons, especially Miss Naomi. Small books began to appear in Evie's basket to join the few that Mama read her at home. As Daddy read her Miss Naomi's book on the cabin's small porch where a breeze would softly brush her face and crickets sang their chirping songs, she wondered if she would make new friends if she searched among the hills, such as at Betsy and Tacy? Would she find Tom Thumb on his adventures? And if she dug deep enough in the small garden, would she find the Fattypuffs and the Thinifers? That made her concerned if she ever found them—would they be a little scary like the lions in Daniel's den?

'Georgie' had come into his own over the last year. Going from a tiny tot to a toddling boy who was the spitting image of Daddy. Though his curiosity found him intrigued by more things than Evie ever was and apt to cause him to be confined to a chair for a short period of 'pouting and tears,' he was gentle and sweet in nature—as was Evie when she toddled on the smooth poplar floors. It didn't take Georgie long to enjoy the days spent at the Jacksons alongside Momma and Evie. First, in a sling on Momma's back, to being placed in a large crate with several other babies, to taking staggering steps across the barnyard. He also learned to like eggs, especially soft and scrambled, but never to the extent of Evie's affection for them, so there was still more for Evie like before, and that made Evie's face bright as a yellow buttercup.

The nights on a low cot in her corner of the tiny mountain home brought sounds that comforted Evie, such as the whippoorwill's songs on a summer evening or the warming crackle of the fireplace fire on a cold night. But the sound that made her young heart feel concerned, though not sure of what, was from Daddy. Because the sounds Daddy made couldn't be good, for the coughing made Daddy grasp for breath, and more than once, a tin bucket caught vomit that caused Daddy's body to shake, leaving him clutching his chest, to then collapsing on the sagging rope bed he and Momma shared. Even at four years of age, Evie knew something was awfully wrong.

In the late summer of 1943, when the first cool winds of fall blew across the mountains, Daddy took sick, unlike how he had ever been before. He was in more pain than usual, and the times of snuggling for a Bible story or just resting in his caring arms became less and less. He would rub his arms and legs for long periods, and Momma would try to smooth his discomfort with the pale green salve she made from the few herbs of lavender and mint she grew in their speck of a garden, mixed with wild white clover. Along with boiled willow bark for pain, Daddy had barely made it through the days of summer to still eke out a meager amount of money, though the days were becoming less and less as Daddy struggled to make the walk up and down the mountain to the mine.

But on a particular evening, as the sun set over tall pines and old maples, Daddy collapsed into a heap on the narrow porch and, even with Momma and Evie's help, was never to rise up again.

Evie ran almost as fast as the cool wind that blew across her face on a path that was worn down with wear and that Evie knew would take her to Miss Naomi, who would know what to do. As she ran, every thought she had only made Evie more fearful. Finally, panting and trembling, Evie arrived at the house she knew as the source of her wonderful eggs. Knocking at the door, amid talk and laughter coming from a home filled with 11 children, somehow Evie was heard. There stood Miss Julia, followed by Miss Naomi, who rushed by her sister to take Evie in her arms. Relief flooded Evie's pounding heart that instant. As Evie spoke through tears and soft babblings, Dr. Alden grabbed his vet bag, giving instructions to Miss Naomi, along with a few siblings, to take Evie home and another one to saddle a horse to fetch Dr. Grant, MD, while he rode on to the cabin that held those that made up Evie's precarious but precious world.

What awaited both Doctor Jacksons was a good neighbor whose body was broken in health and spirit and who knew another day for Wynn Ashby on his beautiful mountain was not to be. The father and son doctors knew the injuries that many could only see externally were a mangled cover of internal injuries from the accident and the unseen disease from the gulps of black air that provided life in an underground pit and that no medicine lay in their small brown bags that could rescue Daddy from many a coal miners fate.

Arms lifted Daddy upright and settled him gently against the cabin's porch wall as Momma crawled beside him and placed his head in her hands. Calling to Evie and Bertie, she kissed his face and told him heaven would be more glorious this time of year and what a sight it would be. Then, taking the children in an embrace, they all leaned closer to hear his last whispers of "Goodbye, my lovelies, till angels call you to me..."

And with that, Evie's beloved Daddy closed his eyes in death. It was said that Momma's voice of wracked pain and sobs could be heard for miles across the mountains, but Evie didn't know about that, for her hands covered her ears to block out Momma's screams and Daddy's last words.

Three days later, on a sunny but chilly afternoon, Daddy was laid to rest in the small church cemetery in the town of Sandy Creek, marked by a handmade cross that Elder Harper had carved, and where in swaying spring and summer wildflowers graced the grave, and in winter branches of holly berries and boughs of white mistletoe rested on the snow, placed by the loving hands of Momma, Georgie, and Evie.

The war ended in June of 1945, but not the one that Momma, Evie, and Georgie fought every day on a mountaintop filled with bittersweet memories and daily hard times. Momma, Evie, and Georgie stayed in the paper-chinked wood cabin and survived by the grace of God, the love of neighbors, and the support of Miss Naomi—who adored Evie and Evie her, who made sure there was food for the table, warm clothes, be they hand-me-downs, odd jobs that earned a few dollars, and of course, eggs. Evie grew strong, beautiful, and 'sharp as a tack' over the next few years and with a heart that was slowly renewed with simple and small joys.

In the late summer of 1952, when nature was beginning to think of fall, with flowers fading into soft colors, leaves on the weeping willows turning to deep golds, and the call of the jar bugs and katydids became a low hum, life for Evie changed as it never had since Daddy died. Momma was getting married, and so was Miss Naomi, and it shook Evie's world to her core!

Momma had met a gentleman, a widower who had moved to the community to run the new service station with the big letters of ESSO on the sign, which was owned by Dr. Alden Jackson and his brother, Roy. Doctor Alden and Roy knew the local little town that was beginning to come back to life after the war was ready for a business of this kind, but because Doctor Alden was still attending the births of calves and administering pig vaccines, and Roy was now a foreman at the new True Temper plant in Charleston, they knew they could build the business but not operate it. As chance would have it, in a coffee shop on the west side of Charleston, having lunch with fellow plant workers, he was told of a man who had lost his wife and recently his job, and with a small boy, needed a new start. Over a party line for eight homes—though no one would listen in, out of respect for his veterinary concerns—Doctor Alden checked the man's references and arranged an interview, where he finally met the man himself.

Doctor Alden, always an excellent judge of the character of a person and the good criteria of livestock, told Roy he thought Mr. Hayes was exactly what they were looking for in an operator of their new establishment. At the local general store in Sandy Creek, in a quiet corner around an old oak barrel covered with worn checkers, Doctor Alden, Roy and Mr. Hayes begin a discussion that outlined the running of the Esso station and salary and ended with shared stories filled with laughter, life, and loss. It began as a business partnership that would grow over time into a friendship that would last a lifetime.

So, on a cloudy, warm Tuesday in late May, with little fanfare but lots of busy and nosey friends and neighbors that came from all over the area, Mr. Hayes opened the door to the new business with the oddly spelled name for all to visit. And in a small rented house, he ate a quiet dinner with the small boy known as Gene on their first night in their new home with sadness but with gratitude to God.

Sunday followed that first Tuesday after a busy and good week of work, and learning of the country church that set off the Pocatalico River Road, Mr.

Hayes took the hand of the beloved boy, walked up to the pretty white building, and entered the Sunlight Baptist Church, not knowing that his life would soon change one more time. On this warm and blue-sky spring day, a Dinner on the Ground was being held on the Davis farm next to the little church, of which the man and the boy were invited to partake. Leaning on a 100-year red oak tree with the boy seated on the ground at his feet and a plate resting in his hand piled high with fried chicken, dumplings, potato salad, home-canned corn and green beans, homemade pickles, and a hunk of cornbread, he scanned the yard full of kind and caring people, and there saw Momma. Momma, with her straw-colored hair like Evie's, a slenderness from years of hard work, a face with a caring smile, and the aura of a gentle loveliness, flipped Mr. Hayes' stomach in a way the fried chicken didn't. Momma didn't notice him at first, but when one of the church ladies slightly nudged her and said she thought the new ESSO man was mesmerized by her, Momma looked his way, and for the first time since she saw Daddy all those years ago, felt her heart stir with unexpected pleasure.

The days and weeks that followed that brief encounter were like a wild whirlwind, and though Evie knew there was something in the air that she couldn't quite put her finger on, she wasn't prepared for the day Momma set her down and told her that Mr. Hayes had asked her to marry him. She explained her how their lives would be changing, but her love for Georgie and Evie never would. Though engulfed in Momma's arms earlier, she lay in her bed that night, and for the first time since Daddy's death, her heart was filled with old and new fears.

The end of summer would soon bring the return to school, which Evie had grown to love. Going to school opened up a landscape of learning that she could not have imagined, though she tried through the books of Momma's and Miss Naomi's. But this year, Evie's thoughts were elsewhere. She knew this change in Momma's life would also bring a change in her life, and not even her beloved books and friends at school could bring peace to comfort her. Evie and Momma's work at the Jacksons was still needed, and every day, even after the school started its yearly adventure, Evie walked to the farm that had nurtured and sustained them for so many years.

On a hot September day when summer was proving it was still in charge, Miss Naomi led Evie to a shade tree near the barn and garden, where a pitcher of cold water awaited them, where Miss Naomi and Evie rested on a large fieldstone, and where Miss Naomi told Evie she would soon be leaving the farm and hollow that had brought Evie so much comfort and joy. Miss Naomi had met a gentleman from another county at a church revival some months before, and love had blossomed when Miss Naomi was beginning to think it would never come to her. She was now to marry 'my love,' as Miss Naomi softly referred to him, a handsome Hank Davidson.

Evie, at the age of 14 years, knew she should be happy for Miss Naomi, so putting on a smile and wrapping her arms around Miss Naomi with a big hug, Evie listened to Miss Naomi's future plans with a sinking heart. Sending her off with a basket of her grand eggs, Evie cried blinding tears along a path she knew as well as the back of her own hand. Stopping under a gently swaying sycamore tree, she sat and waited until her eyes and her heart could stop hurting.

October came to the hollow of Little Sandy Fork as if knowing Evie would need to be consoled by the colors of a brand new # 8 box of Crayola crayons. With every shade of green, orange, red, and yellow, the hollow was ablaze with beauty that made even Evie's heart feel wavering sparks of happiness.

On the first Sunday of the month, after morning preaching, under the 100-year-old red oak tree where Momma and Mr. Hayes first saw each other, Momma married Mr. Hayes. Among family and friends with Evie, Georgie, and Gene by their sides, they softly said their 'I do's,' followed by rounds and rounds of handshakes and back-slapping. And with tables heaped high with church vittles of every kind, joyous songs strummed by Elder Young on his old Martin guitar, conversations filled with ancient wedding tales and laughter, and an amber sunset fading into a good night, even Evie allowed her fearful heart to feel joy.

But that joy was tested when, on the third Saturday of October, Evie shared a pew with Momma, Mr. Hayes, Georgie, Gene, and family and friends from miles around as Miss Naomi married the love of her life. Though the weeks since Momma's wedding had proven to not be wholly horrible, as Evie thought they would be, Evie still had a heart that ached at the changes in her life. She still had Miss Naomi to visit with, where Evie shared the ramblings of her worried heart and Miss Naomi would listen patiently and offer words of comfort and send Evie home with a brown bag of eggs. But even this consolation was now ending, as Miss Naomi was starting a new life. Evie stood with the others, packed into the little Sunlight Baptist Church on another golden fall day, as Doctor Alden Jackson led Miss Naomi down the narrow aisle to stand next to the man she would pledge her life to.

In a ceremony that seemed so brief, and in the big front yard of Doctor Alden and his wife, Etta, where a warm fall sun shone through falling leaves, a splendid dinner of wonderful eats, with jigs, singing, and twirling under the trees, where gossip and laughter filled the air, and the day seemed to short, with Miss Naomi seated in a car covered with tied-on boughs of colorful fall flowers, Evie stood with a cheering crowd lining a dusty road.

Throwing rice as Miss Naomi was carried off, Evie watched until she could no longer see Miss Naomi through teary eyes. Evie's spirit sank like a moss-covered rock into a muddy river bottom.

On a cold, overcast November day, Evie could barely make herself move, and every task she helped Momma, Mr. Hayes, and church folks with was a struggle of such willpower that Evie thought she could not bear another moment and would flee as fast and as far as she could into the surrounding dark woods. For, on the day, Evie was packing the only life she had known into tattered boxes and old crates and watching as Momma and Georgie and all the things she loved most were being taken from her mountain and placed in the little rented house of Mr. Hayes. That evening, after family and friends had left, with boxes stowed in corners, beds made ready with layers of Grandma Viola's quilts, and a warm dinner had been eaten, Evie sat in the small rocker of her first-time own bedroom and wept softly as she did on the day she told Daddy goodbye. Through bitter tears, she wondered what her strange and unwelcome world would bring.

As God scribbled our unseen futures on His drawing board of life, he was placing in Evie's future a happiness that she would have never dared to dream of. Momma and Mr. Hayes made a wonderful couple with a wonderful home of joy, laughter, hard work, love, and continued dedication to God.

As the business with the big ESSO sign grew, so did life for the Hayes'. Momma and Mr. Hayes had a baby girl the following winter, and much to Evie's surprise, she was as thrilled as could be! This sweet-smelling, towhead addition was followed by a move to a larger home, purchased by Momma and Mr. Hayes, and where they would live till the end of their years, filling it with precious memories for Evie, Georgie, Gene, and Sandy, who was named for the little creek that ran by the Sunlight Baptist Church where Momma and Mr. Hayes first met.

In May of '56, Evie graduated high school and surprised even herself by earning a scholarship to a college in Morgantown, West Virginia, an accomplishment that made Momma so proud and made Evie see possibilities that she had never even thought of. She loved the only life she knew among the mountains of a small county town, but something sudden beckoned, and though not sure what it was, she walked toward it with butterflies in her stomach and eagerness in her eyes. But once again, Miss Naomi entered Evie's life, and this time, she shared with Evie more than her glorious eggs.

Miss Naomi and her 'love,' Hank Davidson, had moved to Morgantown, building a life there modest success through hard work and love—but with a heartache that nature seemed to give them in spades. For, time after time, Miss Naomi was unable to carry a child—until this year, on a blistery day in February, when a small and ever-so-plain baby girl came into the world, one who would bring great joy to Miss Naomi and Hank's lives. It was a difficult birth, and only time would prove that no other children would come to this union. Hearing of Evie's grand news of college, Miss Naomi invited Evie to live with her, her husband and the baby, who had now 'plumped out and become awfully pretty' as Miss Naomi lovingly and laughingly said, to a bundle of soft, wiggly roundness. Evie was overjoyed and actually pinched herself at the thoughts of college and time again with Miss Naomi and sharing marvelous eggs at Miss Naomi's table! So, Evie, with Momma's grateful thanks to Miss Naomi, moved to Morgantown and into Miss Naomi's home, and there enjoyed some of the happiest years of Evie's life.

What followed for Evie and Momma, Mr. Hayes, Georgie, Gene, and Sandy were blessings from God that would touch their lives forever. Momma and Mr. Hayes worked diligently at the business with the big ESSO sign, eventually buying the property along with a diner and small market that had come later, before the aging brothers no longer desired to own the business. Within the passing years, the admired and endeared Doctor Alden died unexpectedly of a stroke, and his brother, Roy, retired to his farm, after years at the True Temper plant, to raise the pretty spotted Ayrshire cows.

A future for Evie, Momma, Mr. Hayes, Georgie, and Sandy was one filled with bittersweet events of the past and present that no life can escape—but it also offered a comfortable and generous life far beyond the old mountain cabin of the long past. In retrospect, Evie knew why she was so fearful of her life changes long ago. But now, she knew that God's blueprint—for her and those she loved—laid out tomorrows that would be okay, no matter the ups and downs.

In June of 1960, Evie graduated from West Virginia University with a degree in English, brought about by her love of the stories read by an oil lamp to Evie by Daddy and Momma from the Bible and the little books that were laid in Evie's egg basket by Miss Naomi. In the fall of the same year, Evie moved to Clarksburg, West Virginia, for her first teaching job, one that lasted for three years, which she greatly enjoyed. There, she was still near to Miss Naomi and the green-eyed, curly-headed, chubby girl that Evie had grown to love dearly until an unexpected letter arrived.

Back in Sandy Creek, after services one Sunday at the Sunlight Baptist Church, Momma spoke with a small pride of Evie's hard work at college and present job to a neighbor, who in turn spoke to a cousin, who again, in turn, spoke to an uncle. Before long, an offer was dropped through the post office slot, asking her if she was interested in a position at her childhood high school, which Evie was greatly surprised to receive and immensely excited at the idea. With a week of decision-making and encouragement from Momma, Miss Naomi, and Hank, Evie accepted the job of teaching English literature, and after a long goodbye to Miss Naomi that was filled with streams of tears and promises of many visits, Evie returned to Sandy Creek and to those there she loved beyond measure.

God's blueprint for Evie held much more, as in May of 1964, Evie met 'my love,' as Miss Naomi would have said. On a warm September Sunday afternoon under tall, graceful willow trees by the side of the Little Sandy Creek, surrounded by family and friends, with Preacher John reading from a tattered Bible of many years of use, Evie grasped the hands of a tall and auburn-haired Mr. Donnie Stewart and pledged her life to him till death do they part. Once more, a Dinner on the Ground followed, and once more plates were piled high with food, and once more timeless wife's tales were told, and once more laughter rang up and down the hills and hollows of the Sandy Creek, and once more there was Miss Naomi to share in her day. Evie and Mr. Stewart moved to a nearby town that was closer to the sprawling city of Charleston, where Mr. Stewart opened and owned a successful hardware store, and Evie continued to teach and share her love of literature.

Evie gave birth to a baby girl, followed quickly by another baby girl, both with Mr. Stewart's auburn hair and Evie's hazel eyes with brown nugget centers. Bringing a smile to Evie's heart was her tiny girl's love for those wonderful eggs. And also bringing a smile to Evie's heart was that Evie could step out every day from her kitchen into a backyard filled with maple trees and the grandest chicken coop anyone had ever seen. With her old cherished and frayed pink and green basket gathered delicious eggs, where around a large wooden table over plates of big white fried eggs, Evie told her girls of the days with Momma and Miss Naomi in the barnyard of clucking chickens on Little Sandy Fork.

The years moved by like the second hand of a watch, ticking along with it all the joys and sadness that accompany our paths to dying. Georgie would grow into a tall, handsome man who looked so much like Daddy that it took Evie's breath away at times. He would go to Marshall University in Huntington, West Virginia, becoming an accountant, marrying a sweet girl whom he met at college, and giving Momma two more grandchildren that Momma and Evie both enjoyed abundantly.

Gene took over the business with the big Esso sign, which now read Exxon, married a kind and gentle girl from Roane County, West Virginia, helping Gene to run the businesses and giving Mr. Hayes three grandchildren. It was a grand total of 15 that gathered through the years for noise and enjoyment of birthdays, holidays, and the loud cheering of each other for life's small and big events.

Momma and Mr. Hayes would grow old together until the Thursday afternoon when Mr. Hayes, placing a gentle kiss on Momma's forehead, strolled to the little backyard garden with a small bucket to pick paw-paws from a tree they had planted together so many, many years ago, and fell to the ground in a quiet death. Mr. Hayes was buried by Gene's momma in the old city cemetery with large poplar trees to shade the graves. Momma grieved for Mr. Hayes with deep sorrow, but the true love of her life lay in the small family cemetery on a mountaintop above the Sunlight Baptist Church, and where one day, Momma would lay next to Wynn Ashby, the first love of her life. Momma followed some ten years later, walking through the door to heaven, but before that day, Evie's heart experienced a hurt that would linger forever.

On the fourth day before Christmas of 2010, Evie's phone rang, and sorrow tore at Evie's heart while she listened as Miss Naomi's daughter shared the news that Miss Naomi, while reading her Bible, opened to Isaiah 40:31, "But those who hope in the Lord will renew their strength. They will soar on wings like eagles; they will run and not grow weary, they will walk and not be faint," with pictures of 'her love' and her precious daughter and grandchildren nearby, Miss Naomi had nodded off with a gentle drop of her head to meet eternity.

Other than the time Evie told her Daddy goodbye, Evie had never felt such unbelievable anguish and, in a moment of pure grief, slid to the floor with arms wrapped around her knees, weeping till she could weep no more. The thought of a world without Miss Naomi was one that Evie could not grasp. Evie had already planned her annual holiday visit with Miss Naomi, and a bright red wrapped gift, Miss Naomi's favorite color, lay as a testament to that on a front door table.

The funeral took place four days after Christmas, with Miss Naomi resting at the front of the Sunlight Baptist Church with branches of pine, picked by Miss Naomi's grandsons from a mountain field, lay atop a soft white casket, which Evie thought was as perfect as the smooth white eggs that had brought Evie such pleasure and Miss Naomi into Evie's life.

On that bone-chilling cold December day, with the church filled to overflow, and those who couldn't get inside sitting in the many, many cars in the churchyard with windows down and heaters cranking out hot air, where all listened to the preacher's moving words, and the congregation sang beautifully Miss Naomi's favorite hymns. As the casket was carried to a horse-drawn wagon of Miss Naomi's request, to be laid atop a mountain in the Jackson family cemetery, mourners of every age said a bitter and final goodbye to one of the grandest souls to ever live.

Evie parked her car at the bottom of the road that climbed up to the cemetery and was undrivable in February. Pulling on a pair of boots and drawing her coat and scarf tighter around her body, she started the half-mile walk to the top of the mountain where Miss Naomi lay with her ancestors.

It was hard at first to cast her eyes on the headstone, as it was with Daddy's, because for Evie, only seeing the engraved date made the loss of Miss Naomi real. With warm tears and between sobs, Evie finally told Miss Naomi goodbye, something she couldn't bring herself to do at the funeral, sharing words with Miss Naomi that Miss Naomi couldn't hear but that would have brought to Miss Naomi's beautiful face a sweet smile if she could. Kneeling by the gray granite headstone, Evie unwrapped Miss Naomi's Christmas gift. Under Miss Naomi's name, she laid something that had changed her world forever and had come to symbolize joy and friendship and love, and there she gently placed an egg of glass in beautiful cream and brown speckles...

GARLAND

"The best hearts are ever the bravest"

- Laurence Sterne

The side of the mountain was washed with a wave of morning sun that slowly crept down toward the valley and the Pocatalico River, where a little white house set among century-old oaks and a lone weeping willow. And in that house, in the early sun of a softly lit room, a small wail was heard, and from the country doctor to everyone waiting anxiously, a rush of relief was heard among the hills and valleys at the news of a safe delivery for mother and child. For previous endeavors into motherhood had not been successful, and this once again attempt was accompanied by baited breaths and prayers. As it turned out, the babe born this day would seem to open the floodgates of Iris' womb, and five more healthy babies would grace the home of the Rhodes in the future.

For, on a warm July morning of 1921, after a long night of labor, a baby boy was laid in his mother's arms. Delicate and small in size, Iris Jackson Rhodes took one look at the tiny dark-haired, blue-eyed newborn, and thinking of her own summer birth with her summer name and of the flower chains she made as a child, she pondered for only a few brief moments before announcing he would be called Garland John Rhodes. And though he would love to work in the soil and raise fine gardens during his 88 years of life, it would be an event when he was a tender 13-year-old that would make him a family hero and be given a nickname that would follow him throughout life with pride and laughter.

As the years moved along at the pace of a young silver maple, so did Garland. Sparce for his age with gangly arms and legs, short in stature until his teen years, and not a spare ounce of fat anywhere on his lanky body, Garland's lack of a hefty farm boy's body did not deter him from attempted feats of roughness and toughness at every stage of development. From the days of toddlerhood to early manhood, he enthusiastically plodded along, trying to keep up with siblings and cousins, and though many attempts would fall short, it never discouraged Garland from trying to carry the biggest armload of firewood or chasing a fat hog for butchering, or trying to pull the lead of 1700-pound mare draft horse back to the barn when all she wanted was that field of clover at the other end of the pasture.

But what Garland lacked in muscles and bulk, he made up for with a spirit that was cheerful, funny, gentle, kind, soft-spoken, and a fine singing voice. Sitting in Grandma Mamie's lap at the age of three, Garland would join her in the old negro spiritual 'I'm A-Rolling' with a sweet small voice and dimpled small hands turning round and round. Later, as a teen and young man leading Sunday worship hymns and Wednesday evening prayer meeting songs at the little Sunlight Baptist Church, Garland never dreamed his love of singing would serve him wonderfully in life.

But it was the incident as a lad of not many years that earned him his life-long nickname, which he said many times throughout life helped him to think of himself in a positive light that shined courage into his mind and soul forever.

On small knolls sat farm homes, barns, smokehouses, and gardens that overlooked the bottom fields of a wide range of growing crops. The product of these fields would go to feed the Rhodes, Jacksons, Jones', and many other families' livestock, while the large yard gardens by every farmhouse would go for summertime meals, canning, stocking winter cupboards, and helping neighbors in need.

All the Jackson children and grandchildren, such as the Rhodes, Clendenin, Shamblin, Lowe, and more who were still living at home or on nearby farms, or city relatives who took a day off to help, along with neighbors, would gather during harvest season to work each farm as the crops ripened over various times. It was a time of back-breaking work in the sweltering heat but filled with periods of much-needed rest in the shade of large oak, maple, and beech trees, with pitchers of sweet icy homemade lemonade, along with the latest gossip and boisterous laughter with kith and kin. It was during one of these days in late August that Garland would outshine the adults and bigger children working that day. Growing for months under a hot summer sun, the tall cornstalks filled the fields of every farm and lay in wait for the gatherers and the mule and horse-driven wood wagons. With some stalks as much as 12 feet in height, the corn stood first as growing green shoots and on to tan sentinels in the fields that served as homes for summer creatures and as shadowy figures on moon-lite foggy nights.

Starting at the end of a 200-yard field and lining up at 40 rows across, men began to swing large, sharp scythes, followed by women with curved sickles', and finally by others with pitchforks, as row after row of dried cornstalks were cut down and lifted onto the wagons waiting for the harvested crops. Not much would happen except for the occasion family of rabbits who had sheltered and bred in small tunnels under the protection of growing corn and who would flee with bobbing white tails, scampering for safer fields and nearby woods. Singing ballads and hymns—from Al Jolson's *'Swanee'* to Jimmy Roger's *'T for Texas,'* and a spirited version of *'Swing Low-Sweet Chariot'*—the cutting and the pitching of the corn took on the synchronized rhythm of a choreographed routine, with harmonized singing echoing up and down the hollows and valleys.

It was during this sweating and singing that a high-pitched scream was heard that stopped everyone in their place, and as it happened to be, the scream was near the corn stock that Garland was working. Turning and looking about ten feet behind him, with pitchfork still in hand, Garland, as well as the others, stopped totally in their tracks to take in the scene of eight-year-old Opal, who stood just a few feet from a mass of hissing and slithering rattlesnakes with tail rattles sounding like a hundred maracas. Knowing not to move, for many lessons of farm and mountain living were taught from the cradle, Opal stood still as those around spoke softly among themselves as to what they should do.

Time seemed to stand still as eyes were riveted on the snakes and Opal, when for reasons he never could fathom over the years, Garland, in a moment of fearful distress, rushed forward as if with the feet of angels, past the entangled mass of terror and, pushing Opal out of the way, began to stab at the hissing and striking snakes. As the snakes began to crawl out and over the field, parents, aunts, uncles, cousins, and friends came out of their stupors and, with yells of anger, with scythes, sickles, and with pitchforks, laid to waste to a great number of the poisonous threat in one fell swoop. As pounding hearts slowed down, adrenaline receded, and soft prayers were said for the deliverance of Opal, someone shouted over the quiet, "Thank the Lord for our brave Garland."

Praises begin to be said, and with pats on the back applied, Garland felt for the first time in his life a small pride in himself that he had never felt before and knew he had truly earned. In a moment of sheer joy, Garland ran and, stepping on a wagon wheel, leaped upward onto the corn wagon, and with his bony arms pumped outward with a fist in one hand and his pitchfork in the other and on skinny legs straddling the crop in a fit of pure fun with the brightest smile he could muster, Garland proclaimed to the world, "I'M THE BRAVE CORN CUTTER!"

It was a day of answered prayers, with no one being bitten and a small girl hugging her cousin's neck with gratitude and love. The tale of Garland, Opal, and the snakes spread far and wide and would be retold by family and friends for years to come.

Life moved on from the days of cutting corn, and in the spring of 1939, Garland graduated from Sandy Creek High School, and no one was surprised that his sharp mind would lead him away from the farm and family. Moving to Charleston, West Virginia, Garland could barely wrap his head around the fact that he was going to Morris Harvey College on a fully paid scholarship where he would study music and fulfill what he was sure would be an impossible dream.

Amazed by life on campus, Garland savored every avenue of education he found that was greatly interesting, along with a life where he felt fully accepted as himself and no longer felt a need to prove he was a strapping farm boy like his cousins. But finally growing to a height of 6'1" and adding some pounds to his slender frame from what he called 'college cookin,' Garland needed not to fear, for he could now hold his own when he went home during harvesting and would swing those scythes with high and wide. He also began to catch the eyes of many of the college females and found himself thinking of marriage.

In particular, marriage to a Vivian Fietz. Only two months older than Vivian, Garland worked at getting to know Vivian and getting his nerve up to ask her out for dinner. He had as many classes with her as he could, listening to her chat with other students and picking up on over-heard details, such as she liked fried pork chops and rum-raisin ice cream, was scared of thunderstorms, and loved walks in the snow and dogs of all type. So, in September of 1941, Garland asked Vivian to dinner at the Sherman Restaurant, where, over plates of crispy chops and bowls of cold ice cream, Garland learned that Vivian had been studying him, too.

After two more dinners of their favorite foods at the Sherman Restaurant and the Quarrier diner, they both knew they had met their perfect mate, and plans for the following May wedding were on the horizon. But unknown to them, war was also on the horizon, as was the discovery of a broken heart of a non-romantic nature. Garland had yet to be called for the draft, which the US enacted in October of 1940. But a letter appeared in early March 1942 that would cause considerable consternation for Garland.

At the draft office in Charleston only a few weeks later, after filling out paperwork, Garland, who was hardly ill a day in his life, was taken aside and told he needed to see a specialist. Without an explanation, Garland was given an appointment for the following week, during which time he, Vivian and his family pondered what was happening. At his visit with the specialist, Garland was given an ECG and a fluoroscope, and after waiting for some time while on pins & needles, was told that his heart had a hole in it and that he would not 'qualify' for military service and that there was at the present time no medical aid or cure for his problem.

Garland was discouraged in a life-altering way, disappointed as he had hoped to serve his country, as were many of his siblings, cousins, and friends.

But even more so, he was fearful for what the future would hold with Vivian and his life. Assembled from far and wide, a family gathering was held at Grandpa Grant's and Grandma Mamie's home. Garland, along with Vivian, learned of the issues that could have changed his path in life. As the doctor of the family, Grandpa Grant, MD, shared his thoughts, along with details from the specialist, and with others tossing out their opinions of Garland, the conclusion that was derived, too, was that life should be lived as Garland and Vivian had planned and leave the concerns and the future fate into God's hands.

With prayers said for them and a round of coffee and pie shared, Garland and Vivian returned to Charleston and back to daily living—before a war and a heart problem had sidelined them. So, on a soft blue-sky, sunny Friday in May 1942, in St. Albans, West Virginia, in the small office of a Church of Christ preacher with only his wife as a witness, Garland and Vivian spoke vows of love and devotion, and did just what their families advised, taking a leap of faith and jumping right into living life.

What followed that day in May of 1942 was a marriage of comfort and happiness that endured for 58 years with more wonderful memories than they could count. Garland and Vivian finished their studies at Morris Harvey, with Garland earning a degree in music, and Vivian, a degree in Home Economics. Settling in the small river town of Kanawha City, West Virginia, in a slate-roofed house that rested on a high bank above the Kanawha River, they built a life that surprised everyone, for many feared that Garland's heart would deny him that life. But it did not.

The heart with a hole worked just fine, as did Garland at what he loved best—after his beloved Vivian. Starting at a small grade school, he taught little ones a love of music while returning to Morris Harvey for a graduate degree in choral and director of music. Vivian began her teaching career at South Charleston High School in South Charleston, West Virginia, where she would remain until her retirement, teaching skills from frying eggs to stirring up the creamy white sauce and sharing with female and male students alike the rewards of a tasty meal. Hanging up her many aprons of various colors with big pockets and sometimes trimmed with wide lace, Vivian said goodbye to a career of 43 years that brought her pleasure and love from her students and now cooked only for Garland, their families, and friends, with scrumptious meals that could make a grown man weep. Remembered long after her time of teaching and after her death, with great fondness and laughter, fun tales were shared at class reunions for years to come of exploding blenders, snap beans wars, flaming pans of macaroni and cheese requiring a fire extinguisher, and a rogue pigeon that flew in a window and made off with a ball of biscuit dough.

As for Garland, his life surpassed even his own expectations. At a grade school in Marmet, West Virginia, Garland would begin a career that brought pleasure to generations of students and the community of Kanawha County. Training the young to sing and the singer to improve, Garland, with his rich baritone voice, would guide the voices of hundreds over a lifetime of encouragement and teaching. Beginning at that small country school in Marmet and at a small eastside Baptist church in Charleston, Garland's beautiful direction of voices, great and small, began to be noticed. From one place to another, he was asked to direct choirs and teach classes of singing, proving that from those days on Grandma Mamie's lap, Garland had a gift from God.

As the years went with the swiftness of a magician's hand, Garland would come to direct the student choral at Morris Harvey College, his alma mater, teach and direct a music program of various performances for George Washington High School, and guide the 120 incredible voices of the choir at the Baptist Temple. He could not believe his privilege to work with the best and the most gifted singers over a 45-year span in the town of Charleston, West Virginia. And how those he directed felt just as privileged to have studied and trained under the guidance and tutorage of Garland. His gentle and calm soul never showed anger at anyone bumbling a song or failing to hit the correct note. His laughter at himself, and the gentle poking's of his students or fellow singers, only earned him incredible admiration and love. Sometimes, as he listened with pride to a glorious rendition of a song, he felt that the hole in his heart would fill with joy and then burst with pride.

Both knew that the time together was something that faced us all if given a granted life on this earth. They had enjoyed the days of youth with its fulfilled plans, and they savored the days of aging together with walks by the river, watching a chilly rain sweep across the Kanawha valley as they snuggled in a porch swing, and lunches of cheese and pickles and strong coffee under a pin oak tree planted eons ago in the backyard, but the world tosses out plans with a different ending. Garland said goodbye to his beautiful and adored Vivian in the Lord's year of 2000. After an illness that seemed so unfair to someone with a 'perfect' heart of caring and love, Vivian died of cancer in his arms in the bed that they had shared for a lifetime. Laid to rest on a warm September day in the corner of the Spring Hill Cemetery, near a long-ago placed bench worn with time and visitors, where Vivian, in repose, waited for Garland to come and set and mourn the love of his life, which he often did.

The house they had made into a home and had hoped to fill with the children that were never to be born was filled instead with pictures of family, friends, and their wonderful students, now held a future that Garland did not think he could endure.

But endure he did for another eight years. Siblings, cousins, friends, and former students filled the home with visits, with his favorite oatmeal raisin cookies, joy, laughter, and sweet sounds of singing that he thought the old house would never partake in again. Garland never wandered to sights hither and yon but did venture every Sunday to church to worship a God who had given him a glorious life and to partake of hymns with the raised voices of other believers, to grand and soaring concerts at Charleston civic center, and to performances of the grandchildren of the children he taught so many years ago, and where he would shut his eyes remembering the past, listening as the music and voices of small children in simple verses of childish songs, to the rise of a multitude of a breathtaking crescendo that filled his soul and the auditorium at Morris Harvey College Choir with an amazing grace from God.

Garland began to notice in 2006, though, he told no one, that his body did not seem to work like it used to, and life was getting more difficult with each new sunrise. He seemed to be thinking of Vivian and his childhood more often and, many times found wetness on his cheeks from a memory that had been stored away and forgotten and briefly replaced with new ones. He would eat a minuscule lunch on the small porch that overlooked the great Kanawha River and smile at the memories of the days of swimming in the little Pocatalico River or roaming the hills for the bright red teaberries to make tea, and times with family and friends, of which so many now rested in the earth.

Taking his cane, which was hand craved from an old limb of a soft maple by his cousin, Rafe, he would slowly stroll the little yard, where the gentle, orange-striped tabby 'Ginger,' who ruled the house and made Garland and Vivian laugh with catnip-induced antics, was buried among the oak leave hydrangea, and where beds were filled with Vivian's favorite flowers that she tended to as if they were her children, and that Garland would bring a rose to his face to embrace its sweet summer scent.

It was after these ramblings one evening in 2008, as Garland sat in his favorite old chair that knew the contours of his body so well, when he picked up a picture from the small table that held his Bible, songbooks that he would sing from with an old man's frail voice, and family pictures. He picked up a photo taken by Vivian of a time when Garland was standing on a high stage with his arms held out, directing a performance; he laughed a laugh that he hadn't enjoyed in ages, for it made a grand memory to be recalled and where Garland, standing on an old corn wagon with out-stretched arms, could still hear his words that day an eternity ago of, "I'M THE BRAVE CORN CUTTER!"

Holding the picture next to his chest and letting the weariness of old age cause his eyes to close, and his mind drift to thoughts of Vivian and the past, Garland, in the early morning hours of summer, took a last breath of life and rested a voice that surely the angels will welcome home.

REBA

"How mutable are our feelings, and how strange is that clinging love we have of life even in the excess of misery!"

- Mary Shelly

Reba Ellen Jackson was born on a sunny April day in the year of 1918. And Reba Ellen Jackson came into the world with as little effort and with as little fuss and as quiet as a baby could, as if she knew the world couldn't take another moment of cries or turmoil. With a head of wet curls and a tiny body of five pounds and some odd ounces, she opened her eyes of doe-brown, and with the astounding look of a wise cherub, she charmed all those around her and was snuggled to her mother's breast. With the empty knowledge of a newborn, Reba had no idea that 1918 was to be filled with a war of carnage and devastation and a pandemic that respected no race or status, bringing with it the wastage of 50 million people, though blessedly much of which passed over the small mountain town of Sandy Creek, West Virginia.

Reba, on that day in 1918, was born to Dr. Alden and Etta Jackson, among a large extended loving family who worked the mountain land and a father who tended to the care of animals, which brought no great wealth but did provide a comfortable home, plenty to eat, laughter, joy, and a satisfactory bit of money. Reba would look back in old age and be as sure as she could be that from the day of her conception, the pieces of her life's puzzle never seemed to fit as they did for her brothers and sisters. It was as if the corners had been bent or cut off and wouldn't arrange together as they should. She had heard the stories of her unusual birth that didn't compare with those of her siblings, which consisted of a squalling fight to enter the world that probably made them strong.

For, the gentle and sweet Reba, who possessed the strongest of a beautiful heart, was weak in lacking the physical strength of the others and would live a life of afflictions that accompanied Reba from her beginning to the time of her death. Also, unknown and lurking in the background would be the companionship of incredible joy and incredible misery.

Reba was a small woman of 5'1" with acorn-color hair and dark gray eyes the color of a stormy sunset. She was born with the slightest hump that seemed to grow bigger over time. With each setback or illness, Reba Jackson would be 4' 9" by the time she would lay in a simple maple casket. With steady conviction, Reba, through the long years of tears and fears, had always held to a strong faith in God and a solid hope in life. But by the early middle point of her days, she knew that life had let her down and was afraid that God would, too.

Reba's first illness came at the age of eight months when scarlet fever arrived in Sandy Creek via a traveling salesman who fell ill while bringing the newest gadgets, tonics, and toiletries to the small-town drug store. The salesman lived to peddle his wares another day, and though the disease visited the town of Sandy Creek and the hills and hollows along the Pocatalico River where Reba's family and others lived, none in the community died, which was astounding, with most having mild cases except for Reba, who developed a less serious case of rheumatic fever, that caused no life-threatening problems but did result in a minor heart condition that would accompany Reba for life.

For Reba, a gentle and soft-spoken tad of a girl protected by siblings older and healthier, the dangers of life seemed to come to the frail, small girl more than most. At the age of 26 months, when she jumped off of a bed to show her big brothers that she wasn't a baby anymore, Reba broke her leg, and when not being carried on her brothers' broad shoulders for the next weeks, she hobbled around like a short-legged pirate, much to the amusement of her siblings.

Summertime meant sunshine, juicy raspberries, plump apples, ripe peaches, and fieldwork. Though the fieldwork yielded haystacks for fun climbing, it also brought with it concerns to all who labored in the mountaintop meadows and low valley fields. Because mounds of hay and rows of corn hid mice, rabbits, and snakes, on a hot day as a four-year-old Reba carried a small galvanized bucket of water and a long-handled dipper to her siblings and farm workers, a snake trying to untwine itself from thick hay, sprang forward, striking Reba in the ankle. Crying out softly in surprise, her siblings ran to her and, upon seeing the twisting black serpent, killed it with a pitchfork and gave a brief thanks to God that it wasn't poisonous. Carrying Reba to the house where Momma and a visiting aunt would clean the wound, bandage it, and rock a teary-eyed Reba to sleep, all would be secure in the fact she wasn't seriously harmed. Reba would always be reminded of that day, for she bore a small pale-red scar for life.

Reba Jackson's childhood continued to suffer afflictions that her siblings seemed to avoid, and her body would bear the markings of those events from the first of scarlet fever to appendicitis, to a dislocated shoulder, to a car accident that resulted in many broken bones, and surgeries and treatments for various maladies. But Reba took all of the things life threw at her with courage and patience, never losing her naïve sweetness or joy for living. But that was to change, and Reba would have to dig deep and find the spiritual strength that had never been really needed before but would be for what the future held.

On a trip to Charleston, West Virginia, with big brothers Owen and Orion, Reba leaned out of the old black Model A pickup window, watching the goings-on of the business being conducted at the Charleston City Equipment & Farm Store. It was a trip that Reba loved to join in on, as the town buzzed with activity and people, all of which she found entrancing. On this particular day, a young man of medium height with a shy smile, hair the color of caramel-colored taffy, and broad shoulders toted bags of feed and tossed them in the back bed of the truck, all the while watching Reba. Looking at each other, something felt different than ever before, and each was caught off guard at the fast beating of their hearts.

On the way home, Reba softly inquired of the fellow with a shy smile, only to learn he had also quietly asked about her. Reba could hardly believe her ears and sat silently on the drive home, pondering this new feeling in the pit of her stomach. A feeling that would change her life forever.

For, on a warm and humid day in August of 1937, at the age of 18 years, Reba Jackson became Reba Carter. In the little Sunlight Baptist Church that was set in a valley a few miles from Sandy

Creek and with family and neighbors, Reba could hardly believe that Jacob Carter would be sharing his life with her from this time forward and where a world of dreamed happiness lay before them.

After a reception in Daddy and Momma's big yard under a massive oak tree and showered with handfuls of rice, Reba and Jacob Carter were driven to the train station in Charleston, where they would board the train to Hawks Nest State Park. And in a small room with a stunning view of the New River below, they honeymooned. Sharing dreams of future plans for a family and a home, all built on a relationship with God, Reba and Jacob walked the surrounding hills, vowing to return in the years ahead to the magnificent sunsets over the New River.

Life for Reba and Jacob started out as good as it could be for a young couple from the hollows of Kanawha County. Jacob's job at the feed store provided a steady income, and Reba's new job at one of the recently opened Kroger grocery stores that had sprung up in Charleston since 1926 provided the savings they would put away every week at a branch of the Kanawha Valley Bank. In the fall of 1938, Jacob was promoted to assistant manager at Charleston City Equipment & Farm Store. Reba was promoted, too—this time to future motherhood—having discovered that there was a baby on the way, which filled Reba and Jacob's hearts to the brim with joy!

April of 1939 brought spring showers that soaked the earth for the daffodils that were popping out their yellow heads, and also popping out was a 7 lb. 11 oz. baby boy, who made the Carters a family of three! With taffy brown hair and eyes so blue that the color of a summer sky couldn't match them, James Jacob Carter—'Jamie' to all except his Momma when he was in trouble—was such a charmer that aunts and cousins would line up to babysit the quiet, smiling babe. All were sure a future of only good things awaited the delightful boy who was the apple of his parents' eyes.

That fall, with enough money saved, a small white wood-clapboard house was purchased on a rise on Beech Avenue on the growing west side of Charleston, and it didn't take long for the four-room house to begin to be filled with new and used furniture, toy cars, and a swing on a front porch that provided views of sunsets in the summer and snow falling in the winter.

Rumors of trouble rumbled through the country as a war was stirring in Europe that brought concern to all. But life continued, and with unease in the back of minds, day-to-day living moved at its usual pace. Jacob was busier than ever, it seemed, what with people ordering, buying, and stock-piling for what the news from overseas told them. Reba continued at Kroger, with grandparents and relatives eager to care for 'Jamie,' who was growing as fast as July corn.

More happiness was added to the Carter household when, in September of 1941, a fat baby boy of 8 lbs. 6 oz. was delivered to Reba and named Robert Randall Carter. A wiggly bundle of dark brown hair and dark brown eyes would be known as 'Bobby,' and he was beloved by all, especially his big brother, Jamie, who was sure Randy was his personal pal and would be forever!

The war had arrived in the United States on Dec 7th, 1941, when planes from a little-known land attacked American ships as they lay in a far-away harbor, killing so many of America's 'boys' that the nation was in shock and tears and knew that what small peace that had laid within the shores of the United States for almost a quarter of a century was gone. As with wars of nations, men must fight, and men must die, but for the love of family and country, men drove, rode horseback, and walked to register for a fight they did not ask for and did not want but would battle along fellow countrymen in an entity a thousand miles away.

Along with hundreds of other West Virginian men, Jacob Carter walked into the army's enlistment office at the federal building on the east side of Charleston, and raising his hand, swore to defend his county against all foreign enemies and then walked home with a mixture of excitement and a sliver of fear on his mind. Reba met him at the door and, seeing the enlistment papers in his hand, threw herself into his arms with a heavy heart but one that was so very proud of her Jacob and men like him.

The two weeks before Jacob Carter was to leave for training was a blur of activities for himself and Reba. Suddenly, all the home projects had to be completed, leaving everything in good repair for Reba and 'his boys.' He made sure that Reba would be cared for by family and friends, and all volunteered to help in any way possible, easing Jacob's mind with great relief. At work, he placed his job in the capable hands of old Jasper, who was deemed too aged to fight in a war but still young enough to be Jacob's replacement till Jacob returned home to his sweet Reba and boys, which he prayed would not be long in coming.

Reba prepared herself for life without Jacob by learning to drive their used but good-running Chevy sedan, learning to replace window screens, learning to mow their little patch of grass and balancing household accounts. She had many more odd things to learn, and that list would grow as time passed without Jacob to lean on.

On a cold March afternoon with their small boys in tow, Reba and Jacob rode to the train depot in silence with only the sound of the car's heater and the sweet mutterings of Jamie and Randy softly talking to each other. As they parked and walked to the train station, they were surprised at how many men, women, and children were already there to say goodbye to each other. Soon joining the awaiting families, they noticed the low tones of loving utterances and flowing tears that each family shared. What seemed like only seconds to say goodbye, Jacob felt his heart pound with sadness when the conductor yelled, "All aboard!"

Engulfing Reba and his boys in his arms and whispering words of love and a brief prayer, Jacob, along with 16 other men, climbed aboard the C & O Railroad that, connecting with other train lines, would eventually take them to the state of Washington and to Camp Lewis.

Reba Carter returned to a home that was lacking the complete joy that only a few months ago resided in unmeasurable quantity. But Reba knew that though her days, weeks, and months ahead would hold extra hard work and longing for Jacob, she would not be facing what her gentile and kind husband would be enduring to prepare for war and then to march into it. So, Reba straightened her shoulders, tied on her apron, started dinner, and knew she would endure till Jacob returned.

The letters from Jacob Carter began to arrive quicker than Reba imagined and brought such happiness and comfort to her heart. She read them to Jamie and Randy, and though too young to grasp all the words, the boys were enthralled by the papers held in Momma's hand.

Reba continued to be employed by Kroger, and with the loss of so many men to the various and needed military jobs, with the boys in the care of family, Reba Carter filled many jobs at the store and rose to the position of department manager. This not only added income but brought an extra busyness that, in a small way, eased Reba's loneliness.

By late summer of 1942, the letters from Jacob came 'far & fewer,' and the year seemed to slow and linger as if lost in time, and the war that many thought would be over quickly dragged on with no end in the foreseeable future. The few anticipated letters that did appear in Reba's mailbox told Reba that her Jacob had arrived in North Africa—and what a shock the land was to him. He said that for a mountain boy used to tree-covered hills and valleys of green to a land of blowing sand, intense heat, sparse scrub bush, and wind-driven hills of moving dunes, it was *"a sight these eyes have never seen and a place I'd rather not be."*

On a beautiful 1942 November day, her sons played in the small backyard with her sister Celia's sons. She and Celia enjoyed a cup of hot coffee and Celia's homemade cinnamon rolls and laughed at the antics of four small boys. Unknown to Reba, at a government building some miles away, two men in their best and pressed army uniforms, holding a piece of paper that had arrived only an hour earlier, had climbed into their plain-looking car and began the arduous and somber drive to the little house on Beech Avenue. The car pulled up and parked, and the officers walked up the front steps and knocked on the door. With no answer but hearing the sounds of children, they proceeded to the rear yard, and there saw the idyllic scene that made their guts churn because they knew how this family's world was about to change. Celia's boy, Roger, saw them first and, pointing, asked his Momma who the men were.

As both women leaped to their feet, their hearts sank, for both husbands of the sisters were serving in the military, but Celia knew that the men standing in front of her and her sister were not there to carry a letter to her. Reba Carter knew, too, and before she could fully process the sight, she collapsed to the ground with a twisted face of truth and tears that came as fast and brutal as a sleet-encrusted blizzard. Celia fell down to Reba's side to comfort her, at which an onslaught of small boys ran to her in wails of fear and arms wrapping around her body.

The officers also moved to the sides of the two women and slowly lifted Reba into a chair. Taking charge, one of the officers suggested that Celia take the children inside, and with the aid of the second officer who directed and carried the smallest boy, a weeping Celia slowly trod into the little house, looking back only once and seeing the pained Reba, looked away in heartache.

Reba Carter sat in stunned quiet, with anguish she didn't think she could bear in her heart and with her mind in a sickening jumble of thoughts and pain. The officer sat in silence with Reba, and only as she noticed the paper in his hand was a word spoken.

With a throat constricted by sobs, Reba asked what the paper said, and though she knew it would tell of her Jacob and not truly wanting to hear, Reba had to know. The officer, with kind eyes and a gentle voice, read the words from the Western Union Telegram to Reba.

"Mrs. Reba Carter, it is with deep regret that I inform you that your husband Sgt. Jacob Carter, USA, was killed in action at Oran, Algeria, on November 9th in the performance of his duty and service to his country. Please accept my heartfelt sympathy. Lloyd R. Fredendall, Major General of the USA."

Reba Carter, who had known a life of illness and mishaps, was coming face-to-face with an anguish that she never thought would be felt in her heart. So overwhelmed that she didn't know what to do, and she sat motionless in disbelief. Reba took the telegram from the officer's hand and, with her eyes staring straight ahead as if looking beyond the heavens, shut her eyes and turned aside in a heap of grief. The officer raised from the chair and walked softly to the back door of the little house and, entering, asked Celia if there was anything he could do, but only a quiet "No, thank you" was the reply.

As the two officers left the small kitchen and walked away, they both regarded Celia with four small boys either in her arms or at her knees, and Reba in a curled ball of anguish rocking in a soft green painted metal lawn chair, they made their way back to the car with faces that said it all. That war truly was from hell, and their jobs were on the road to it.

A knock at the front door of the Beech Avenue house brought Celia out of shock, and opening it to Edith Garrett, Celia fell into Edith's arms. Edith Garrett knew what the black car with two army officers meant, knowing from the experience of WW l and the loss of her beloved husband, Paul, and had come to tend the hearts of the two sisters, especially Reba and her boys, whom she had come to care for greatly. Celia motioned toward the backyard, where Edith Garrett quietly walked to, where she took Reba into her arms, and where muffled cries were wept onto Edith Garett's shoulder. News soon reached the family and friends of Sandy Creek and Charleston, arriving in waves and with gentle hands, led Reba through the next weeks of loss and living.

Reba was stunned to learn that Jacob would not be returned to her until after the war, and knowing for the sake of her boys that life had to go on, Reba clung to Jesus' yoke laying her burden upon Him, once more accepting the fates of life with a buried inner strength. On a cold January evening on the tiny front porch overlooking the town below and wrapped in her and Jacob's wedding quilt, Reba stood alone with a sigh of acceptance, knowing she would face a future of uncertainty without Jacob by her side but with God's help she could handle 'come what may' with strength from God. Reba Carter would discover that even His strength was almost not enough.

March could be a beautiful month and March could be a brutal month. But mostly, March was a month of confusion, as if it had lost its way from the previous March, not knowing what to do with new days. So, as each March dawn appeared over the mountains, it either entered gently with sun-drenched soft warmth or swept in with wild winds of bitter wet cold, leaving the land and those that lived there as bewildered as the month. Today, it had chosen to be dark and frigid and to shroud the little Sunlight Baptist church in a cloud of soulful despair that matched the hearts in the old, worn pews. And today, for Reba Jackson Carter, there was very little about March 1943 that felt even remotely redeemable.

For, in the middle of the little country church, resting on painted pale-white saw horses laid a small, unadorned, unvarnished maple casket that had been built with care, and on that casket lay a woman's hand that gently rubbed the smooth maple edges as if to comfort the small body of an 18-month boy who couldn't win the battle when pneumonia invaded twelve days earlier.

Reba Carter could barely take her eyes off of 'Randy,' and though she wanted to push a wisp of his sandy brown hair backward, she couldn't bring herself to move her hands from the coffin. And though she wanted to lay his favorite blue and white puppy blanket over him, she couldn't bring herself to walk across the room to gather it for him. For to do so, in her mind, was abandonment. How could she leave him now, and how could she leave him later when they lowered him into a grave on a windy and frigid mountaintop? And how could she offer comfort to the slender boy of four years who stood by her chair with fear and bewilderment on his face, who would no longer play with toy cars, or share a cookie, or be followed around by his adored baby brother?

The truck of Jacob's former boss, washed and polished and with boughs of pine branches and holly entwined on the front bumper, led the procession from the Sunlight Baptist Church to the top of a mountain where generations of Jackson's laid. Reba, with Jamie on her lap and her father's arm around her, stared in silence as she watched the road in front of her that would lead to Randy's small grave. Following behind in trucks and hay wagons, a gathering of mourners filled the little cemetery to comfort and support Reba as best as they could. The hills and valleys echoed the hymn *Resting in the Arms of Jesus* as the body of a wee boy was laid in the cold pit, and Reba Carter cried out for the first time, truly believing that her heart would die in her, too.

At her side stood Jamie, and even at four years old, he knew the world he loved so dearly was changed, and grasping Reba's hand tighter and leaning his head onto her arm, wept tears that no child should ever have to weep. Reba and Jamie stood by the small grave until everyone had drifted away and, tossing in an early spring crocus', bid Randy goodbye. For the first time in her life, Reba wasn't sure she could bear one more day of loss, and she would wander off to a solitary place, lay down, and die like a wounded animal.

But the sun did rise for another day, and it was hard for Reba to leave her body from the bed that she once shared with Jacob and that now held and comforted a little boy who had cried into his pillow every night for weeks now. Reba would sing Jamie songs and stroke his hair, and only then did either one find a troubled sleep. Reba's life was slowly turning its way toward some sense of normalcy, and Jamie made it happen whether Reba wanted it to or not because a four-year-old needs stability that Reba knew she would have to provide.

Reba Jackson Carter's family, Jacob Carter's family, and a few close friends stood on the sidelines, and with their help, Reba returned to work at Kroger, and Jamie began to smile when a cookie and a snuggle were offered. Reba and Jamie developed a new routine that included pancakes on

Saturday mornings, dinner at the corner diner before Wednesday night church, a visit with flowers to Bobby's grave on a warm Sunday afternoon, and snuggles in the front porch swing as a storm rolled across Kanawha valley, and so by the end of the summer of 1943, Jamie was closer to being an active little boy, and Reba could breathe without her heart about to shred to pieces. A sort of peace had come to the little white house on Beech Avenue.

On October 10, 1947, the first army ship, the USAT Honda Knot, landed in Oakland, California, carrying 3,027 caskets as a military band played *'Taps'* and Verdi's *'Requiem.'* Inside were the remains of Americans who had died in the Pacific— the first to be repatriated from the battlefields of World War II. From 1947 until 1951, more than 171,000 bodies—60 percent of America's World War II combat dead—were brought back from 86 countries on six continents. The remainder were laid to rest in permanent overseas cemeteries.

It was on a cold November day in 1948, almost to the day that Jacob Carter died, when a knock at Reba's door shook her world once more. Unbeknown to Reba, a train in the dark of night quietly stopped at the C & O depot, and there, along with 9 fallen soldiers, the casket of Jacob Carter was unloaded. Military trucks and funeral home cars waited in silence for the families to arrive and claim their loved ones. The officer that morning asked if she was Mrs. Reba Carter, and

Reba knew from that day in 1942 that it would not be good news. The paper said her Jacob was home and awaited her at the depot that overlooked the black-blue waters of the Kanawha River and where she had told Jacob goodbye those short years ago.

Reba thought once more that things in her life would never stop hurting, and leaning into the door frame, she prayed for strength once more. Taking Jamie by the hand, Reba walked next door to Edith Garrett's and, using Edith's phone, called her father and mother to come to her for support and to drive her to claim Jacob's body. So, Alden and Etta Jackson, along with their daughter, Reba, and grandson, Jamie, stood under black umbrellas with little relief from the pouring rain that had begun to fall only an hour before. In the gloom of the day and through hard raindrops, Reba walked to Jacob Carter's simple wooden casket and, through a wall of tears, signed a paper that would finally give Jacob back to her.

Four days later, the Cunningham Funeral Home carried Jacob's body to the Jackson Cemetery, and once again, on a cold, windy mountain, Reba Carter watched as the beloved body and part of her heart were lowered into the ground. With Jamie by her side and with her family and Jacob's following, Reba walked off the mountain for what she hoped would be the last time for a long time because she felt she couldn't take more blows from a life that seemed to want to knock her forever in a despairing down. With prayers and trust, once more, a pattern of living resumed, and life seemed to ebb and flow with what little joy could be snatched.

In the late spring of 1950, life for Reba and Jamie would change once more, and it seemed for a brief time, it would bring an essence that both would savor and find happiness in. For, on the day, entering the Kroger office to speak to the store manager about a new product he was sure the store would want to offer to its customers was a man who immediately caught the eye of Reba and all of the staff in the surrounding area.

Wayne Schroder was a man of striking good looks, height of 6' 3", a toned 220 pounds, wavy dark hair, intense eyes of chocolate brown, a 100-watt smile, and an air of possible danger. Sweeping the room slowly, as if looking for a long-lost friend, Wayne Schroder's eyes finally settled on Reba, and walking to Reba's desk, he stated, "I believe Mr. Dovell, your manager, is expecting me," while all the time never taking his eyes off of Reba.

Years later, Reba would know those eyes were looking for a 'particular' type of woman, one of naivety and meekness, and how she unknowing was what he was seeking and wanted that day in 1950.

Three days later, as Reba Carter waited for the bus that would take her home, there near the corner stood Wayne Schroder. In a starched light blue shirt and a pair of creased navy worsted wool pants, and with that smile, Wayne strolled over to Reba and, ever so politely, asked if he could drive her home. Overwhelmed by the attention and the odd sensation in her stomach, the fact had never crossed her mind that she would be attracted to another man after her Jacob, yet Reba Carter softly said, "Yes."

Climbing into a sleek pale blue car, they barely spoke on the drive home. Reba invited Wayne to a glass of iced tea on the front porch, and there they spoke a little of themselves. Wayne said he knew some about Reba, as he had already asked a few folks at Kroger about her; he seemed thoroughly interested in the rest of the story about herself, Jacob, and her boys. Wayne shared that he was 37 years old, was a long-distance truck driver for R. E. Harper Trucking for almost 20 years, owned a little farm on Dutch Ridge Road outside of Charleston, and had never been married but hoped someday to have a wife and family.

When Reba gave him a quizzical look, he said, "I've been in a few relationships, but I've never met the woman that could share my life, though I think that's about to change."

Reba smiled as her mind took in this man, and her heart skipped in her chest. And looking out over the valley, could not believe that life might be sending her happiness again. Wayne took her hand, leaned over, placed a kiss on her cheek and, raising to walk off the porch to his car, said, "I think lady luck has smiled on us today," and he drove off.

The knock at the door on a warm Saturday morning a week later caught Reba by surprise, and following Jamie to answer it, she was thrilled to see Wayne standing with a bunch of spring flowers. Reba invited him, introducing him to 11-year-old Jamie, who was confused by this unknown person but knew what this man and his flowers probably meant. Wayne asked if they were free and, if so, would they like to spend the day with him, going to his little farm for a picnic. Turning to Jamie for his approval, who slowly nodded his head up and down.

Reba also said, "Yes, we would."

Grabbing her purse, old shoes for her and Jamie, and light jackets, Reba locked the door and, following Jamie, seated herself in the sleek pale blue car.

The farm on Dutch Hollow Road consisted of 30 mostly wooded acres, a pretty and well-maintained farmhouse in a cream color with pale blue shutters, a small barn in the same color, a tiny garden, and a four-acre spring-feed pond. Reba was not prepared for the clean and nice interior of the house but was pleased, for to her, it spoke a lot of Wayne Schroder. A walk around the farm showed walnut, maple, oak, and mountain laurel trees, a barn that sheltered an old but well-cared-for tractor for mowing, a pond stocked with fat basses, perch and sunfish, and a new well that provided water to the house.

Under a wide maple, Wayne served up fried chicken, potato salad, green beans, cornbread, apple pie, and bottles of cold pop he had purchased at the little local country store. With that 100-watt smile and a coy look, he admitted he had only made the cornbread, with his sister, Irene, fixing the rest of the meal. Reba and Jamie both laughed, but Reba was overcome with a feeling that this man could bring true joy into her heart again.

Three months later, on the front porch where they sat in the swing and talked for the first time, Wayne Schroder asked Reba Carter to marry him. Having Jamie join them, sharing Wayne's request, and getting Jamie's approval, she said yes.

In the old rock-face stone Kanawha County courthouse in the late summer of 1950, with Jamie by her side, she and Wayne held hands, said their 'I dos' to the justice of the peace, and signed a certificate that would bind them for life.

Reba had asked Wayne to drive them two days later to Sandy Creek, and so on a humid Sunday afternoon in August of 1950, Reba, Wayne and Jamie pulled up in front of the old Jackson farmhouse, where Reba knew most of her family would be after morning worship for a day of laughter and meal-sharing, and to the surprise of everyone, introduced her new husband. Silence fell like the stillness of falling snow, and for several almost tangible minutes, no one spoke among her loved ones, but catching a tear of joy in Reba's eye and seeing Jamie's big smile, Reba's mother rushed to Reba's side and embraced her with a hearty congratulations. Brothers, sisters, aunts, uncles, and siblings followed suit, and the rest of the day was spent learning about future plans and sharing in Reba's new happiness. At about 7 p.m., as the sun began to cast long shadows across the hills and valleys, many started to their own homes, and so did Reba, Jamie, and Wayne.

As they drove off, with Jamie hanging out of the car window yelling bye to everyone, silence once again came to the Jackson porch. And finally, in a voice of concern, Reba's brother, Owen, said, "I'm not sure why, but there is an uneasiness in my gut that tells me I should be worried about this marriage." And many heads nodded in agreement.

The first two years of marriage were almost more than Reba could have wished for after the losses that still lingered in her heart and soul. Wayne thought it best for them to continue to live in Reba's Beech Avenue house, though at first, Reba felt pangs of missing Jacob when Wayne first shared her bed. But Wayne said due to the fact that he was out of town a lot for trucking deliveries to Chicago, New York City, Atlanta, and Houston, and with Reba still working at Kroger, and Jamie was settled in with friends at J. E. Robbins Elementary School, the little house on Beech Avenue served them best, and surrounded by precious old memories and building sweet new ones, Reba had to agree.

The 'Funny Farm,' as Jamie called it in the first years, was the place where he, his cousins, and friends had fun playing in the woods and fishing and swimming in the pond on weekends. Reba yearned for another child and had always assumed she would conceive more children, as it was something that she and Wayne both wanted, but by year three of marriage, and after visits to various doctors, Reba knew that for whatever reason, children did not seem to be in God's plans for them. And though Reba knew Wayne was disappointed, she did not understand the reason for the changes in Wayne's behavior toward her and Jamie, for she thought the life she and Jamie shared with Wayne contained enough joy for all. But for Wayne, something in him became angry and bitter, not only at the thought of no children, but of the life he thought he could control every aspect of was not to be, and a side of Wayne that was buried and hidden came to a boiling surface.

The first time Wayne verbally abused Reba was over a pie burnt while she was hanging laundry. He attacked Reba with such harsh words and fury that Reba stood in shock. It was not Reba's nature to strike back, and so in a small fear and an eagerness to please, Reba apologized, hoping that was the end of that. But it was not, for a week later, when Jamie brought home a report card with not his usual good marks, Wayne back-handed him, knocking him to the living room floor. In stunned silence, Reba grabbed Jamie and fled to a bedroom, and in the growing darkness of the evening, Reba cried bitter tears and Jamie clinched his fists in an inner wrath.

That day, when his twisted reality came forth permanently, Wayne Schoder turned into someone who was totally unknown to Reba and Jamie, as did their world. The Jackson family could read unsettling signs in both Reba and Jamie, but neither of them would comment for fear that Wayne had taken on new heights, and neither did Reba's family make comments or ask questions until a surprise visit to the little house on Beech Avenue revealed a bruised cheek on Jamie and the curious oddity of the cotton dress Reba was wearing, which made Owen and Orion look at each other and wonder why on a scorching hot summer day Reba was wearing long sleeves.

In a voice that was caring and soft, Orion asked Reba to roll her sleeves up, and though hesitating for some moments, Reba did as she was asked, revealing massive bruises in every shade of the colors of blue and purple. For the first time in their lives, Reba's brothers had malevolent thoughts for another human and said so, but Reba defended Wayne, which did not surprise them as Reba always saw the good in everyone, no matter how vile they were.

Owen and Orion stood quietly for a time to reflect on the scene before them, with Owen saying, "Reba, I hope you leave with us today, but if you don't and choose to stay, know that Jamie is going to leave this house with us, and probably will never return."

Walking to a chair, Reba lowered herself down and knowing her brothers were right, shook her head yes, and buried her tears in her shaking hands. In an old suitcase that had belonged to his great-grandfather, Grant Jackson, many years ago and a slatted wooden box from the back porch, Jamie Carter filled them with clothes, shoes, coats, hats, awards from school, books, his Bible, and a picture of Jacob he kept hidden under his mattress. On that day in 1953, 14-year-old Jamie knew Uncle Owen was right; he would never return to this house to live, and he also knew Wayne would destroy anything he left behind. Owen and Orion carried all of Jamie's worldly goods to their truck, while on the front porch, Reba told Jamie to be strong and take courage as the Good Word says and to take heart that one day joy would come to them again.

After hugging each other and Reba giving a salted kiss on his forehead, Jamie Carter walked away from his childhood home and, waving goodbye to Reba, drove off without looking back for fear his heart would break at her small lone figure watching him leave. Reba knew she could have left with Jamie, as her brothers pleaded with her to do. For she still had her job, and the Beech Avenue house was in her name only, and she had savings hidden from Wayne, but Reba had made a vow before man and God, and she wasn't ready to walk away from the commitment.

Gravel crunched as Wayne pulled into the narrow drive next to the Beech Avenue house, in his purchase that day of a new 1953 Pontiac Chieftain convertible in fire engine red. Reba couldn't believe her eyes when she first saw it because every car Wayne had ever owned was some shade of blue. Reba considered with a wary and furrowed brow what this change meant. Reba had Wayne's favorite meal ready on the stove, knowing he'd be home today from a run to Houston. Wayne hardly spoke to her anymore and mostly ignored her except at mealtime and bedtime, both of which Reba had come to hate but endured out of determination and fear.

Noticing that Jamie was not home but assuming he was off playing baseball with neighborhood friends, Wayne spoke nothing of Jamie, took a bath, ate in silence, and left, saying, "I'll be back later." And with a quick look back with eyes of malice, he walked out the door.

Hurt and shame rose in Reba for allowing this man to treat her in such a cruel way, but she also felt her shoulders ease and the knot in her stomach go away, for another few hours, Reba would have calm. At 11 p.m., Wayne returned and, taking a quick look in Jamie's bedroom, realized that something was wrong. Turning on the light, he immediately knew that Jamie was gone—really gone. Stomping into their bedroom, Reba feigned sleep, which had no effect on Wayne's rampage, and dragging her from bed, he stood in a seething rage as Reba told of her brother's visit and Jamie's departure. Grabbing her by her neck, Wayne squeezed it and told her only he could have allowed Jamie to leave and that one day, Reba would push him too far. Slamming her back onto the bed, Wayne walked to the refrigerator for a beer, strolled to the front porch swing, and studied the view below while Reba wept herself to sleep.

The next day, while eating breakfast, Reba noticed Wayne seemed to have changed overnight. He looked at her through hooded, menacing eyes, spoke to Reba in a lowered-metered voice, and told her how things were to be; she would be quitting her job to take care of only him, she would never see Jamie again, she would never see her family at any time, she would never leave the house without him for any reason, and the doors of her brief, weekly sanctuary, the little Parson's Chapel, would not open to her again.

Leaning over and waving a fist in the air in her face, Wayne said, "If you disobey my rules, or if I ever know of you seeing Jamie again, or learn that any of your family has been in this house, know unmistakenly, that I will kill Jamie and bury him where you will never find him."

Staring at Wayne, Reba truly knew that Hades was real and the Demon who ruled it was sitting at her table.

In the following days, in a note Reba had slipped to Edith Garrett over the backyard fence, Reba wrote of the changes in Wayne, the fear for her and Jamie's life, and to relay the recent events to her family for them to honor her wishes to be left alone and to raise Jamie in the manner in which she and Jacob would have done. Reba did as Wayne said, and for the next 10 years, Reba lived at Wayne 'beck and call,' living in an undoubting hope and trusting in the promises of prayer that her life would one day somehow change. Reba was kept informed of family news by Edith Garrett. Edith would meet with a member of the Jackson family every few months at a predetermined spot such as the drug store, beauty shop, or Kroger, learning of family updates of births, marriages, and deaths, and of course, news of Jamie, and passing it along to Reba while she hung clothes on the line or walked to the mailbox.

It was also where Edith Garrett passed snippets of information concerning Wayne on to Reba that Reba came to understand much of why her marriage had changed so greatly. Reba felt she had only herself to blame for the life she was living. She knew her loneliness and heartache over the loss of Jacob and Bobby had made her vulnerable, and ignoring her family's surprise and hesitation toward Wayne, Reba grabbed onto the smooth words of Wayne and believed all would be good and lovely, now realizing that Wayne Schroder knew that day in the office at Kroger that Reba was 'his type,' and as bits of information of Wayne's past were affirmed, Reba was the only one who fell so totally under his charms and would become Wayne's greatest triumph.

Wayne knew Reba was staying in touch with her family but was not sure how or when since he controlled her as best as he could by intimidation and fear. He felt Edith Garrett was aiding Reba, but even Wayne knew not to threaten Edith, for she had three sons who Wayne knew could, and would, make him painfully pay for any intimidation toward their mother. So, the cruel years ground away at the pace of an old dripping faucet and where Reba thought she could bear life no longer but instead held on, for the smallest news of Jamie made her see each day with hope.

Jamie Carter thought of his mother every day but continued to obey her wishes and to make her proud. Almost every member of the Jackson family adopted Jamie into their lives, and Jamie spent the last 10 years showered with love, care, and encouragement. Jamie graduated Sandy Creek High School with honors and earned a degree in accounting from Marshall University, where, to his amazement, he went to work for the company that owned several businesses in Charleston, including Charleston City Equipment and Farm Store, where Jacob Carter not only worked but where Jacob and

Reba Jackson met. Along the way, Jamie met a green-eyed, chestnut-brown-haired wisp of a girl by the name of Cate, who reminded him of his sweet mother and whom he knew Reba would love and hoped one day would meet. And where, on their wedding day, he shed tears of joy for his beautiful bride but also tears of sadness for the vacant seat where Reba should have shared in this day.

The farm had become Wayne's place of retreat during the ten years of Reba's imprisonment. He had grown to hate her very being, but his seething hate also refused to surrender to a divorce, and though savoring his time at the farm without Reba, he occasionally brought her along to torment her of the past happiness that it once held. He never worried about Reba leaving him, so whether on the road working or at the farm relaxing, he knew his threats and her fears would keep her in the little house on Beech Avenue.

What Reba didn't know was that Wayne had been in a relationship with Loretta Hawkins for the last ten years of his marriage to Reba. It was her that was on his mind all those years ago while sitting in the front porch swing at the time Jamie was taken. He knew then that there really wouldn't ever be children of his own, and even though Jamie had been a constant reminder that he might not be 'the man' he thought he was, Loretta made him feel like that didn't matter. A woman 10 years his junior, the divorced Loretta who didn't like long nights alone in a big bed, with two children of her own, a well-heeled ex-husband who paid good alimony and child support and found in Wayne, her ideal companion for the life she wanted to live. And for Wayne, who saw in Loretta his fulfillment as a man while playing step-daddy to her kids and who made Reba look like a worn-out and bedraggled has-been, Wayne enjoyed a wildness he never had with Reba, and with no strings to Loretta, was savoring a perfect existence. The thoughts of Loretta in his arms and Reba huddled at home brought a smile of great pleasure and satisfaction to Wayne's face.

It was the summer of 1961, and at the start of her 11th year of her tormented life with Wayne, that Reba heard the news that hurt her heart yet filled it with such unspeakable joy, for news arrived by her aging neighbor Edith, that Jamie was the father of a baby boy named Jacob and that Reba was a grandmother, but of a grandchild she might never hold!

Reba's world took on new meaning and for the first time ever, a courage welled up in her that she knew she would have to act on, for that baby boy needed to be in her arms, and she had to make it happen. Though it terrified Reba, she began in earnest to plot an escape from Wayne, and once the idea began, her plan played in her mind daily like an old black-and-white movie of fleeing and flight and was to come to bear the fruit of freedom in the weeks ahead.

But life, as it so often does, had its own plan.

At 8:20 a.m., on a hot Saturday morning in 1964, Wayne arrived at Beech Avenue mightily annoyed, angry, and disappointed from the farm where he had spent Friday night without Loretta, and where he now sat on the front porch in vexation over the loss of an evening of illicit pleasure.

Strolling into the house and sliding onto a chair at the small kitchen table, Wayne looked at his breakfast, knocking it to the floor, and in a fit of rage, grabbed Reba by her shoulders and slammed her head into the wall because his eggs were over-cooked, and holding a fork at her throat, told her she better get them right next time or he'd bury the fork in her chest. And for good measure, he slapped her across the mouth, busting her lips where blood, mingled with her tears, began to flow.

Wayne turned, taking his car keys in hand, and heading to the front door, told Reba, "I'm going to the farm, and when I get back Sunday, you best have this mess and yourself cleaned up."

Sliding to the floor in a bleeding and fearful heap, Reba knew her plan to leave had to happen even sooner, as in today.

At 3:20 p.m., on the same Saturday, around the corner from Edith Garret's house on Beech Avenue, Jamie stood still and searched for any signs of Wayne's car. Seeing none, he walked into Edith's yard and tapped softly on a window, almost scaring the old soul half to death. Edith's look of relief turned into a huge smile at the surprise of seeing Jamie.

Quietly talking through the open window, Jamie asked about Reba and Wayne. Edith said Reba was the same as always as far as she knew, and Wayne was at the farm if she had heard him correctly when yelling and leaving the house earlier that morning. Jamie asked Edith to go to his mother's house to see if Wayne was really gone and let Reba know he was coming home for the first time in almost 11 years. Edith quickly agreed and said she would be the 'lion at the gate' to make sure Wayne would not arrive unawares.

Reba could hardly believe her ears when Edith said that Jamie was here to see her, and Edith could hardly believe her eyes at the sight of Reba's battered body. Motioning for Jamie, crossing the yard in large strides, he and Edith stepped on the back porch and out came Reba with open arms and tears flowing so hard she could barely see her precious boy.

After long hugs and kisses planted on each cheek, they both just stood and took each other in. Reba could hardly believe this was her Jamie, but it was—all grown-up and looking like her handsome Jacob more than she ever thought he could. But Jamie was not prepared for what he saw, for his beautiful mother of the past was gone, and in her place was a woman aged before her time, with more gray hair than the soft brown he remembered, lines of a harsh life carved into her once round face, and a small thin body carrying the signs of a recent beating.

Devastated by what he saw, Jamie told her, "Momma, I'll be back to you come hell or high water, and I'll be home to stay," and sliding a tiny picture of his baby boy into her hands, he slipped out and back to his car.

Reba and Edith embraced, and both women knew life was about to change, for prayers had been answered.

At 10:23 p.m., on the same Saturday, life would take a detour for Wayne. But before that 'turn in life's road,' Loretta had returned to the farm, where they had walked the land, fed the fat fish in the pond, had a tryst in the barn's hay, and eaten a supper Loretta had picked up at the Tip-Top Drive-In. Wayne Schroder was in his element and felt life couldn't get much better.

Standing bare-chested and in his underwear at the kitchen sink, Wayne was showing signs of too much eating, too much drinking, too much time in a long-distance truck, and too much time doing nothing else. As he lifted the spoon of his favorite ice cream to his mouth, he wasn't thinking about any of those things.

But as the mantel clock ticked away the fateful time, and where, a few rooms away, Loretta lay on the sofa in the living room, watching Matt Dillon and Chester head for a shoot-out on the streets of Dodge City, Wayne saw the face through the window screen over the sink. For a few seconds, he thought, *I'm going to kill that son-of-a-bitch,* before two bullets from a second-hand .38 Special tore into Wayne's soft gut and instantly wiped that idea away. At first, he just stood there looking straight ahead with blank eyes before he said, "Loretta, come..." and dropped to his knees onto the blue checkered linoleum floor.

Loretta, looking as Marshall Dillon fired shot after shot at a gang of bank robbers, said, "I'm coming", and casually strolled into the kitchen to find a dead Wayne face-up in a spreading pool of blood with a spoon of melting Rocky Road clutched in his hand.

At 10:57 p.m., the police and an ambulance arrived, along with nosey neighbors who said they had heard nothing as they were watching their favorite Saturday night TV shows filled with singers, dancers, shoot 'em up westerns, and a handsome lawyer named Perry Mason. Loretta Hawkins, too shaken to drive, was loaded into a police car to be driven to her mother's house, and Wayne Schroder was loaded into an ambulance to be driven to the city morgue, where he would lay for the next hour on a cold metal slab while the coroner ate his late evening snack of blackberry pie his wife had packed for him.

Looking across the room at the body, the coroner hoped that Wayne Schroder had had a last good day on earth. Wayne probably would have disagreed with him.

At 11:09 p.m., a revolver emptied of ammunition was tossed into the middle of Two Mile Creek and sunk like a stone to be buried in years of mud and muck. It would be snagged on a fishing line, much to the surprise of a father and son, 34 years later, on a too-hot summer day in 1995, when the fish weren't biting, but a silver & black snub-nose gun was. Thinking this might be a sign that a day on the lake was not working out, they wrapped the gun in an old rag and dropped it off at the local police station. The user of the gun who killed Wayne Schoder knew to wear gloves in all aspects of the unfortunate misdeed, and throwing in years of river water and bottom decay, the old weapon would yield no information or clues. It would lay in the basement of the Kanawha County courthouse with a few thousand other items of crime until it was lost in a forgotten bin.

At 7:18 a.m., on Sunday morning, as Reba was sitting at the kitchen table with a cup of coffee in her hand, footsteps could be heard on the front porch. When the screen door didn't open, but instead, the rapping began, Reba knew it wasn't Wayne and wished for a moment that it was the Lord coming to take her home. Answering the door and seeing two Charleston City police officers, Reba was sure this day was about to take a bad turn, and her thoughts and fears came to rest on Jamie.

Stepping outside onto the porch, the men told her that there had been a shooting on Dutch Ridge Road and that her husband, Wayne Schroder, had been killed. Reba had experienced a lot in her 43 years of life that had shaken her to her core, but this one didn't, which surprised the gentle and kind Reba.

Not fathoming at first the words spoken, Reba slid onto the old wooden swing and, staring out across the valley below, wondered if it could be true. In a brief moment of remembrance of joyful days, Reba began to weep for Wayne, but that passed as quickly as water through a sieve, and when an officer sat down beside her and offered her his handkerchief, little did he know that the tears being wept were tears of relieve and of hope! They told her that the city morgue would be in touch with her concerning the body, and as they walked to their car, Edith Garrett stepped onto the porch and took Reba in her arms.

When told of Wayne Shroder's death, Edith looked skyward and, in a raised voice, called out, "Prayers have been answered!"

At 9:10 a.m., footsteps could be heard again on the front porch and walking to the door, Reba saw Jamie. For the second time in 24 hours, her boy was home. Hugging each tightly, Reba settled once more onto the swing, where she shared with Jamie the news of Wayne's death and what she had learned when she had spoken earlier to her cousin, Parris Rhodes, a homicide detective with the Charleston City Police.

Jamie listened intently and showed no emotions as Reba told what happened and that no one knew who or why Wayne was killed. When asked what she wanted to do about Wayne, Reba said she was doing nothing. Jamie was a little taken aback as Reba had a heart of pure gold, but knowing what Wayne had put her through, he understood that Reba was burying in this moment the 11 years of bitter memories for a final goodbye.

Edith, seeing Jamie arrive, delivered fried eggs, ham, buttered biscuits, and a pot of hot coffee and offered to help in any way she could. Over the first breakfast they had shared in over 11 years, Reba and Jamie Carter spoke of a future that held happiness and the thrill of freedom for both.

At 11:05 a.m., Jamie rose to leave after what was one of the most joyful days of his and Reba's lives. Reba took him in her arms once more and, saying how she loved him, walked to the front porch and blew him kisses as he lowered himself into his car.

Starting the car and putting the window down, Jamie Carter sat silently for a few moments with a peculiar look on his face and said, "Remember yesterday when I said I was going to come home for good? I guess life decided to make it happen", and with a soft smile, he drove off.

Reba's breath caught in her throat, and her stomach felt odd because Reba was certain at that moment that Jamie was the one who removed Wayne Schroder from their lives. A shiver ran down her spine, and she knew they would never speak of that telling moment again. And knowing that her mistakes and decisions years ago had led to Jamie's lethal actions, Reba could find no fault in her and Jacob's son.

On a gray day at the Mt. Olivet Cemetery, Wayne Schroder was buried in a cheap pine casket with very few flowers and very few mourners, which did not include Reba or Jamie. Some of Wayne's family thought poorly of Reba Carter, who had done so little for the final resting of her husband, but most knew why she didn't and withheld their opinions.

Later, Loretta Hawkins placed a small plain headstone at Wayne's grave and visited it often. Reba never did. Jamie did once, and with an embittered smile and spitting upon the grave, walked away with a grateful and relieved heart from a world that held no Wayne Schroder.

Unbeknown to Reba, Wayne had a life insurance policy that he had meant to change but never did, and to the amazement of all, had left her $100,000.00!

When Reba received the check, her hands shook, and Jamie went with her to the bank for fear she might faint when she saw her bank balance.

Reba sold the hated farm but was pleased with what it sold for, which added to her 'pay-back fund,' as Edith Garrett called it. Reba paid off the mortgage on the little Beech Avenue house, brought Jamie, his sweet wife, and baby Jacob a home for their growing family in a new area of Charleston called Loudon Heights, and helped Jamie start his own accounting firm with Reba as a silent partner.

But in her final act at Wayne, Reba drove the shiny red convertible to the Mountaineer Salvage Company on the outskirts of town and watched with pleasure as a claw lifted the car onto a heap of steel and a flat iron weight crushed it beyond recognition.

Jamie turned to Reba and said, "I'm sure if bullets hadn't killed Wayne, seeing this would have."

Walking to Jamie's truck, Reba said, "I would have kept the car if it had been any color but blue or red, but it wasn't, and for that, it had to go."

Reba continued to live in the little house on Beech Avenue for another 30 years, reliving the beautiful days when Jacob, Jamie, and Randy filled the house with hugs, laughter, and the bliss of an innocent and unknown future. Everyone told her to remodel the house to help erase some old memories and aid in making new ones, and to her surprise, she did. She thought the new kitchen was wonderful, the central heating system was amazing, the new box-spring bed and over-stuffed rocker good for her weary bones, and who would have thought she could watch her favorite TV shows with color!

The life back with Jamie and her family once more brought lots of changes to Reba's world, and she savored every second with baby Jacob and, later, with the additions of Vinson Robert and Sherry Robin.

Reba asked for her old job back at Kroger, but time had moved on, and her skills were outdated. However, the privately owned Charleston Department Store, which so many of her family and friends shopped at over the years, found a spot for her, and Reba could not believe how much she enjoyed the next 32 years of helping folks pick out the right coat or dress or hair clasp or a tiny pair of shoes for babies first step, and how fast they went by.

But one day, while carrying a basket of wet clothes to the backyard to hang up to dry, Reba fell and lay for 15 minutes in pain, afraid to move. Crawling and lifting herself into a lawn chair and checking that nothing was broken, Reba knew that the autumn of her life was upon her.

That afternoon, with a cup of coffee and a handful of Chips Ahoy cookies and resting on her old porch swing, Reba truly noticed for the first time that her neighborhood was changing. Her dearest friend, Edith Garret, was long gone, as were most of the families that had become friends. New families had moved in and, though friendly, were too busy with living life to connect with the old woman whom they only saw in passing and occasionally waved to. Also, Reba noticed a different atmosphere on the west side of Charleston, as old businesses, such as her beauty shop, were being replaced by arcades and 'hippy' stores. Even the local drug store no longer sold the much-loved little ham salad sandwiches or cherry cokes that had become a favorite treat on many days after work. Reba decided that afternoon, after pondering that once again changes were coming, that she would talk with Jamie for advice and think of a new plan that lay ahead.

After long, thoughtful conversations with Jamie, his wife, grandkids, her siblings, and church friends—after all, Reba was cautious in actions, if nothing else—Reba accepted what she considered sage counseling and started her 'old age adventure' as one of her sisters called it.

Going to work her last week at the West Side Department Store after giving a two weeks' notice, much to her surprise, there awaited a small party, which brought hugs, joy, tears, and pretty packages of little parting gifts that filled Reba with a grateful heart.

Reba's next big change involved her niece, Barbara Jo, a real estate broker, for a different abode seemed to suit Jamie's new thinking, one that would encompass the needs and wants of the elderly woman his momma had become. Reba was blessed with a solid bank account due to good investments advised by her nephew, Stephen Davis, a banker, and dividends from Jamie's successful accounting firm in which she held shares.

Reba thought about what she would miss when leaving the Beech Avenue home, and she knew immediately it would be her front porch and the view of the town below. So, on a whim at Barbara Jo's suggestion, Reba walked into an apartment in the center of Charleston, with a balcony on the 6th floor of a beautiful old red-brick building, which overlooked the dark blue waters of the wide Kanawha River. As the sun reflected off the water, boats idled up and down the slow-moving current, and a little jazz band played old Benny Goodman tunes under a tall concert canopy, with people of all ages savoring a warm late Saturday afternoon. Reba knew immediately this would be her home.

Selling the little white Beech Avenue house was hard for Reba and Jamie, but once her decision was made, and the apartment or condo, as some liked to call it, was bought, Reba was excited and filled with eagerness to start her 'old age adventure.'

Reba Carter found life in her apartment filled with things she never thought she would enjoy doing. Her neighbors, mostly near her age, took her under their wings, and like an eaglet, off she soared to games of bingo and mahjong (*Is that even a real word?* she wondered), trips to the mall for shopping, lunch in tea rooms with names like *The Dusty Rose*, flower shows with exotic orchids, and even to a concert to hear George Jones sing in sweet harmony with Tammy Wynette. But of course, her greatest joy was Jamie and his family of 11, who were regular visitors in and out of her apartment with their stories of school and college, woes or happy tales of dating or losing a football game, and introducing her to pepperoni pizza and eggs rolls and teasing her about not getting her feet wet at their annual summer trip to an ocean front house on a South Carolina beach.

Reba had to pinch herself every now and then at how her life, which had been so bittersweet for so many years, was now an unbelievable bliss that she looked forward to facing every day she was blessed with. Reba was very aware that she had come to the place the Psalmist spoke of in Psalm 90:10: "The years of our life are seventy, or even by reason of strength eighty; yet their span is but toil and trouble; they are soon gone, and we fly away."

As such, Reba thanked God at each new sunrise and at the close of each sunset for the beautiful gifts that encompassed all aspects of her life, which, at one time, would have seemed impossible to her.

With a most grateful heart, Reba knew her time in the here and now was drawing to a close, and peace dwelled within that thought. As the Prophet Isaiah in the Bible told King Hezekiah to "put his house in order," that is exactly what Reba did.

Under the care and guidance of her dear cousin, Cleo Jackson, wills & testaments were made with bequests to loved ones, her church and her favorite charities. The apartment had been signed over to Jamie for years now, as was her assent, and in a small leather-topped desk, a drawer held a list of the keepsakes and the names to whom they would go.

Reba's name on the gray-granite round-top headstone with two hearts entwined together among craved flowers and where she would share an earthly eternity with Jacob, was only waiting for a new and final date to be craved. Next to her and Jacob, set a smaller headstone of marbled white and gray with a little angel in prayer with folded hands engraved into the granite, and that marked the ground that held her precious tiny Bobby. For in death, she would finally be united with the two souls she had loved until her last breath.

On a cool late August day that had been spared the summer heat but had savored an early morning soft rain, Reba sat on her beloved balcony among pots of fat Gerber daisies, bright red geraniums, pink sweet peas, and lemon-yellow marigolds, which were to welcome the coming autumn.

Watching the gentle flow of the wide water that lay before her, bringing to mind the days of a long-ago honeymoon overlooking the New River, with her and Jacob's wedding quilt over her lap, Reba let the setting of the day and the setting of her life lure her to sleep. And on that day, in 2005, at the age of 87 years, Reba left this life with as little fuss and as little effort as the day she was born.

TIM

"A mule isn't just a mule. He is sanity. He is happiness. He is a teacher.

He is a therapist. He is a friend!"

- Western Mule Magazine

Timothy Jackson was a boy with bright red hair and soft red eyebrows, blue eyes the color of sapphire marbles, the personality of a ripe, sweet peach, gangly to the point of being bony, and standing 5 feet and 10 inches by the age of 14 years. 'Tim' to family and friends, he loved just about everyone, including all animals, but especially horses, donkeys, and a beloved favorite mule. And Tim could ride them all with the talent of a seasoned Texas cowboy.

Tim was sharp as the proverbial tack but disliked school because it took him away from his animals and the bottom land acreage that lay by the Pocatalico River in Kanawha County, West Virginia, where he practiced his breakaway roping, as Tim would not partake of a thing that would harm an animal, and where he taught his favorite animal 'Merlin' to do tricks and any maneuver that a rodeo horse could do.

Now, Merlin the Mule, so named after one of Tim's favorite books, *The Story of King Arthur and His Knights,* had magical powers that Tim was sure of because Merlin would hide behind a giant oak tree or a haystack or another mule and disappear, waiting in silence and stillness until an apple or sugar cube was offered—and which brought him running at full gallop, and braying as if proud that he had pulled the wool over on Tim's eyes. Merlin loved Tim from the first time Tim walked into the barn stall as Merlin wobbled on newborn legs. Tim caught Merlin as he was about to tumble to the hay-covered floor with gentle arms and a warm snuggle. And for Tim, that tiny creature that leaned into his arms and cuddled into Tim's chest brought a joy to Tim's heart that would last forever.

Merlin the Mule was not only smart but fast, too, much to the amazement of many, easily bypassing big draft horses and quick donkeys, and even many of the fine-looking equine owned by local men who loved nothing better than to race on a two-mile-long dirt road on Goose Creek on a Saturday summer afternoon, with dust devils roiling up at the pounding hoofs as if Satan himself had placed a bet. Tim had great affection for all animals and, with wonderful care and patience, hand-raised not only mules and horses but also dogs, cats, and even pigs. He was a nature trainer of critters, even to the point that Grandpa Grant told Tim to un-train Grandpa Grant's horses as the animals refused, on many occasions, to obey Grandpa Grant, which could create a problem when the farm hands took to plowing.

Grandpa Grant said he would have no horse or mule that had to have a sugar cube to pull a plow or a winter sleigh, yet Grandpa Grant was mighty proud of Tim's abilities and, despite complaints, carried a pocket of sugar cubes in the winter and pieces of fruit in the summer.

Through the years of growing up and the adventures with his beloved mule, what Tim loved best was to run errands with Merlin over the mountains and up and down the hollows and the valleys that connected all the farms by ancient, well-trodden narrow paths and wide trails. Merlin was as sure-footed as a deer, and even in the rainy season, with mud sometimes four inches deep, his feet stayed steady and grounded, be it on flat fields or a slopy hillside.

Tim, the second child out of eight, was almost always the errand boy for his Momma Delilah and Dad Allen and other relatives when needed. The oldest child was almost always with their father in the fields plowing and sowing, harvesting hay or corn, or in old-growth woods chopping firewood for the cast-iron stove that Momma made mouth-watering meals on or for the pot-belly stoves that kept the cold at bay in frigid mountain winters. The younger children helped in the milking barn with Momma, picking summer vegetables for eating or canning, churning butter, helping in the house, or caring for the babies that seem to come along with a regular occurrence.

Tim joined in all of the farm chores that were needed for family living, but since he and Merlin were the most competent for the task of doing errands, that's what they did on many a day year-round. Most of Tim and Merlin's mountain errands included the mundane tasks of going to Mrs. Davis's to borrow sugar for sweeting teaberry tea, taking an apple pie over to Mrs. McClung when she was down with bursitis, or a load of wood in the fall for old Mr. Monroe, a widower, to the serious requests, such as the times his uncle Alden Jackson, the veterinarian, was needed when 'Buttercup' struggled to produce a calf, or when cousin Nora Ruth needed to be taken to the hospital in Charleston in Grandpa Grant Jackson, M.D.'s car. Everyone knew that Tim was always there to help, was always trustworthy, and was as dependable as the rising of the sun, so the day he disappeared was a day of anxiety and great concern.

It was a hot summer day, and on a winding path lined with red maples, elms, tulip poplars, yellow birches, black tupelos, and mighty oaks, Tim and Merlin were enjoying the cooling shade of those tall, old trees, the gentle gait, and swaying of a lazy ride that was accompanied by a much-appreciated breeze. Tim knew every family, every farm, and every cabin, especially the one that belonged some time ago to his friend, Evie, who he helped to move to the little town of Sandy Creek.

The dilapidated cabin had lain empty for some time, but as Tim approached, he caught a whiff of something unfamiliar that he was sure shouldn't be filling the air in this area of the forest. Rounding a small bend, Tim saw smoke rising from the cabin, and that panicked Tim, for he knew a fire of any kind could set ablaze his mountains, which were dry as a box of old tinder from a summer where only smidgens of rain had fallen.

Tim climbed off Merlin, led him behind a huge sycamore tree, and told Merlin to 'stay,' which Merlin would do. Merlin the Mule could almost read Tim's thoughts like a book and his surroundings even more, as his sense of smell and sense of hearing were both acute and attuned to predators, his stall mates, or Tim. And so, along with Tim, Merlin was feeling something akin to fear, and Merlin knew when told to remain out of sight, he needed to obey and be vigilant.

Tim removed his slightly worn hand-me-down CanVee High Tops and eased his way barefoot as quietly as he could through the thick undergrowth that led to behind the cabin. Squinting through filtered but bright sunlight, Tim saw what was producing the unfamiliar smell and knew that not only was it illegal but dangerous for the woods and wildlife if it exploded or was left unattended. Part of the outside back wall had been removed, with the old hued logs laying on the ground, and near the aged soot-covered fieldstone fireplace stood a contraption that was large and ugly but mesmerizing at the same time.

Tim watched with fascination the two men and one woman working the 'moonshine still' with expertise that must have come from years of distilling. The contraption, connected together by four parts that seemed to take up half of the cabin and most of the fireplace, was a sight to see. The metal drum rested on metal legs in the fireplace with metal tubes coming out the top and running over to three wooden barrels. The barrels were of varying sizes, from small to large, with a few mediums thrown in and ending with a hose dripping into a bucket.

Around the room and on the ground out back stood what seemed like hundreds of little barrels, stoneware jugs, and mason jars. To Tim's thinking, they must have been using the cabin since last fall and had a large clientele, of which Tim was sure even some of his scalawag relatives were imbibers of the pale-yellow liquid that could make your ears ring, your throat burn, and cause a crooked walk.

Resting on his hunches and watching closing for some time, Tim heard a small nay. Merlin was concerned and was wondering where his boy was, and though he remained as told, he felt the need to let Tim know of his anxiousness. What Merlin didn't know was that not only Tim had heard the nay. For one of the men had moved to the small front porch to smoke a hand-rolled 'rolly' and heard it, too.

Tim raised quickly to his feet and, as fast and quietly as he could, darted low in the trees to get to Merlin. He wasn't fearful for Merlin unless the man was carrying a gun because Merlin would kick and stomp anyone who tried to ride him except for those Merlin knew and loved. But Tim was still scared, and even more so as he finally approached Merlin and heard the man on the porch yell out, "Revenuer!"

Tim grabbed Merlin by the mane, pulling himself upon the mule in record time, and turning to the path, headed for help! But the moonshiner was fast, too, and springing off the porch, he covered the beaten-down excuse of a little front yard, leaped over a fallen serviceberry tree, and grabbed Tim with a force that caused Tim to loudly yelp and land painfully hard on the ground. Tim's first thought and concern was of Merlin, and as best as he could, Tim cried out, "Flee, Merlin," which Merlin did before the moonshiner could grab his harness.

Galloping at a run, Merlin headed for a not-to-far stand of wide old pine trees, and there in the midst of them stood as silent and still as Grandpa Grant's wall-mounted 8-point buck head. The man hefted Tim up by the collar and, fending off Tim's fraying arms, dragged him to the cabin porch, where a rope hung and would be used to bound Tim up until the moonshiner decided what to do with him.

The two other purveyors of distillery came running from the back of the cabin and, seeing Tim, stopped dead in the tracks, wondering what to do with a skinny boy who wasn't a revenuer but would bring the law to their door with an unpleasant outcome. The biggest moonshiner, who seemed to be the boss and who held Tim in his grasp, told the others to get the rope and help tie Tim to a post. Still kicking and fighting and yelling, the three of them wrapped the rope around Tim and a leaning post and told Tim that, unless he wanted a rag stuffed in his mouth, he had best shut up.

Then, as they stood at a distance, talking softly among themselves, Tim was sure they were plotting Tim's demise, and for one of the few times in his life, he was truly frightened.

The day slowly began to sink into the evening, and Tim could hear lots of noises, which caused him to ponder what was happening. It didn't take long to find out what those sounds were, for piece after piece of the moonshine-making still, along with jugs and boxes of moonshine, began to materialize and be carried into the woods to be hidden as best they could. Tim sat as still and quiet as he could, in hopes that, with all of the turmoil that Tim's appearance had caused, he would be forgotten. Tim also prayed that he would not be killed, that Merlin would not be stolen, and that his heavenward thoughts would cause his family to come hither and yon searching for him.

Darkness was upon the mountain, but thankfully, there was a half-moon, and Tim could make out the tree area where Merlin remained hidden and unharmed. Tim was taken aback when the woman moonshiner stepped out of the cabin's crooked front door. Fear tossed Tim's stomach as if he had eaten some early spring green apples.

But the woman had kind eyes and, speaking softly, told Tim she had brought him some water and a biscuit. Tim wanted to refuse it, but his throat was so dry that he could barely swallow. The moonshiner held a glass jar to Tim's lips, and as he drank, he almost cried.

The biscuit, though stale, tasted good, and again, tears filled Tim's eyes, and it gave him a glimmer of hope that he might remain unharmed. Holding the jar to Tim's lips once more, the woman rose up and stepped back inside the cabin. Those few moments of kindness and generosity from an outsider, from a person unknown to Tim or from the community that nurtured him, also gave Tim a glimmer of a world that he hadn't experienced before and caused in Tim a desire to learn more of God's giant sphere and its inhabitants, as he pondered his fate on an old cabin porch on a hot summer night.

A low, pale red and orange sun woke Tim, and he sat there in thought as to how the day was going to play out. Before long, Tim could hear movement in the cabin and then came the whiff of coffee carried by a morning breeze. Much to Tim's surprise, the other man appeared on the porch and, carrying a mug, asked Tim if he wanted a drink of coffee. Tim shook his head, yes, and the mug was held to his lips once more. The taste of coffee was wonderful but made him homesick for his momma's breakfast and her old stove-top percolator. It caused him to think of Grandpa Grant and the rest of the family and their frantic thoughts that must be attending them all this summer sunrise.

The man moonshiner set the mug down on the porch and, untying Tim slightly, helped Tim off the porch to a sheltered tree, where he was told to relieve himself. As the man turned to lead Tim back to the porch, Tim heard from the woods a far-off sound of a sputtering engine. The man seemed unfazed by the arrival of a vehicle, so Tim knew it was more bootleggers coming to collect the 'shine' and probably Tim as well.

With his heart racing like the second hand on a pocket watch, Tim knew he had to make an attempt to get home, and with every ounce of courage he could muster, Tim turned, ran, and yelled, "Merlin!"

Merlin, who had been standing by in ponderance silence through the night, now finally hearing Tim's voice, felt something was about to happen, but he wasn't sure what. At first, with soft and slow steps, Merlin moved from behind the trees, following the sound of a man's raised angry voice, to where Merlin could see his beloved owner.

Suddenly, with a gut bray that caused the moonshiner to turn around in shock, Merlin took the last few feet as fast as he could and head-butted the man with such force that it sent the moonshiner tumbling head-over-heel into the edge of the old porch, knocking the wind out of him. Merlin moved closer to stomp the man who was hurting Tim, but Tim grabbed Merlin's lead and yelled, "No, Merlin!" Struggling to free himself from the loose ropes, Tim leaped up as if his legs had springs and landed on Merlin's back, turning to the path for home.

Merlin galloped as if being chased by Grandma Mamie with a big straw broom when he was caught eating her pretty blue coneflowers! Tim could hear voices yelling behind him, but he knew they wouldn't catch him, for Merlin was running as he had never run before. The path ran for miles over the mountains, and it seemed even longer to Tim that day. He knew if he could make it to Grandpa

Grant's, which was the closest farm to the path, he would be safe because there were always aunts, uncles, cousins, and hired help at Grandpa Grant's, and the full force of those protective souls would land badly on anyone who threatened their own.

Tim watched with vigilant eyes for the little narrow track that broke off and led to Grandpa Grant's, and recognizing the old beech tree that marked the track, he slowed Merlin down just enough to make the turn safely. Though only a mile down to Grandpa Grant's, the ride seemed as if it would never end. Then, off in the distance, stood the familiar and loved farmhouse.

It was said that nobody had ever seen anyone with the appearance of Tim Jones when he rode into the front yard of Grandpa Grant on that day. Merlin, with wild eyes, ears laid flat back, and panting like a sprint runner, galloped across the yard with Tim astride on his back, hanging on for dear life. And Tim, with eyes wide as if a specter from the grave was chasing him, his face filled with fear, and his sweat-drenched hair pushed back by the wind and standing up on end, yelled, "Help, they're coming to get me, they're coming to get me!" while reigning in Merlin to a sliding, sod-tearing stop! When Tim jumped from Merlin's back and landed with a knee-bending thud, his appearance was one right out of a comedy horror film, with Grandpa Grant and the others startled and not quite sure what was happening.

And neither did Aunt Elsa as she shouted, "THAT TIM JONES LOOKS LIKE HE JUST RODE A MULE AROUND THE WORLD!" A comment that would be remembered and retold for generations to come.

As folks gathered around him and Merlin, with a cousin bringing over the well dipper filled with water for Tim and a pail filled for Merlin, Tim told his story. Disbelief, followed by anger, took hold of the family, and all knew what needed to be done. Jumping into cars and a few trucks, with horseback riders bringing up the rear, the clan rode to the base of the mountain and the trail that would lead them to the old cabin. Armed with pistols, rifles, and shotguns, they marched as quietly and as fast as they could to the old cabin to confront the moonshiners, but today, there would be no face-off, and many were thankful for the payback over the capture of Tim could have been deadly. What they did find was some sippin' product that was left behind, a 'still' hidden in the woods that would soon be nothing but remnants, never to drip a drop of moonshine again, and Tim's well-worn CanVee High Tops.

Tim's days of riding the mountain paths and trails by himself ended after that adventure. Someone always accompanied him on his missions, and someone always carried a gun. Tim missed his solitary days of going up and down the 'hills and hollows,' running errands and shooting the occasional rabbit or squirrel for the stew pot waiting at home. The adventure that may have scared a few years off of his life did cause Tim to reflect on the tenderness shown to him on that mountain and the world and the people in it, and it came to serve Tim well in later life. He remembered his fear of the large moonshiner who overpowered him, the kind woman who fed him water and a biscuit, and how this example of hardness and softness helped to understand his dealing with men and beasts. Tim returned to school that fall with pats on his back from teachers and friends, who were glad to see his safe return, and for the first time, due to the dangerous time on an old falling-down porch, Tim began to seriously think about what he wanted to do when he did grow up.

Tim loved to read. While perusing the little Sandy Creek town library, Tim came upon a book about the art of training race horses and the farms resting in a Bluegrass State where many of those magnificent equines were born, raised, and trained. Tim researched what he might need to know for training racehorses and began a lifetime of study for a job Tim knew he was born to do.

Tim and Merlin loved going to Grandpa Grant's home to watch that wonderful new device called television, which was one of Grandpa Grant's most prized processions. It was a tan and dark brown table-top GE that sat on a cherished small, oak cabinet inherited from Great-Grandma Viola, who Tim had never met but enjoyed the stories of her gentleness and toughness raising a family in the West Virginia mountains. Tim, Grandpa Grant, and Merlin eagerly awaited any horse races on the small screen, especially the ones at a place called Churchill Downs. They would get so caught up in the races that Grandma Mamie had to yell for them to stop jumping up and down after her daddy's picture fell from the wall, and at Merlin not to knock over furniture as he watched with his head lounging through an open window. The three were a sight to see, and Grandma said many times that she should charge admission to see the view!

Tim graduated high school and, saving every penny he had earned during those years, enrolled at Bethany College in West Virginia. There, Tim learned of equine science, horse anatomy, nutrition, health care, horse physiology, and training techniques from experienced teachers and trainers. Tim was in his element! And waiting back in Sandy Creek were Grandpa Grant and Grandma Mamie, Daddy Allen and Momma Delilah, aunts, uncles, and cousins, all eager to hear of Tim's time at college.

On one of these visits, Grandpa Grant shared with Tim some family history. Grandpa Grant was one of the keepers of the family's genealogy, and while looking through old pages of ancestors one day, recording a new family birth, Grandpa Grant came upon an ancestor by the name of Green. Something about that name rang a bell with Grandpa Grant. It was while reading the

Charleston Gazette about horse racing that Grandpa Grant saw a possible family connection to Jonathan S. Green. He suggested to Tim that in Kentucky was a family that owned acres of gently rolling hills and acres of blue meadow filled with sweet hay and magnificent horses and that Tim should drift that way upon graduation from college.

Climbing off a Greyhound bus in Green Valley, Kentucky, Tim walked the last few miles along rows of white fences and fields of bluish-colored grass and arrived at a place that was something out of those horse picture books Tim read years ago at the little town library. He immediately knew that this was where he belonged. With his heart pounding wildly with trepidation, Tim walked through the gates of the farm and up to a big house, where he knocked gently and, to his surprise, was shown into the study of Marston S. Green, grandson of Jonathan S. Green.

Mr. Green was not what Tim had expected from a famous racehorse owner of many a winning prodigy. But he had a kindness about him, as if he may have sensed the young man's nervousness, and he invited Tim to have a seat and explain his visit. And so, Tim began his story—with the love of a mule named Merlin, the moonshiners who made him ponder his life, a grandpa who hinted at a connection to the Green family, and ending with Tim's shining forth love of horses! Mr. Marston S. Green listened and knew Tim was a man after his own heart. And as such, in the fall of 1958, at the age of 22 years, Tim was hired as a stable hand at Licking River Farm in the rolling hills and level meadows of Kentucky with the most grateful heart a young man could have.

Though a meager salary was offered for starters, which Tim eagerly accepted, his only stipulation was that he could bring Merlin the mule to join him and reside with him on the farm. Taken somewhat aback by Tim's forward request and the fact that his most loved animal was a large, big-eared chestnut-colored mule, Mr. Marston S. Green and the farm management reluctantly agreed and even loaned Tim a truck, a horse trailer, and a driver by the name of Quinn, to transport Merlin to the green meadows of Licking River Farm. What a sight it was when Tim pulled off the little country road and onto Grandpa Grant's farm, where Merlin resided and was spoiled with apples, carrots, turnips, and his own block of salt. Merlin knew instantly who had arrived when Tim stepped out of the truck, and with his best and loudest braying, he called out to his Tim! Embracing Merlin's warm face with its prickly whiskers, Tim nestled Merlin to him and whispered words of affection.

Everyone came from miles around to see the fancy truck with *'Licking River Farm'* written on the side and the shiny horse trailer, loaded with bales of alfalfa hay brought along from the wide meadows of Kentucky—hay for the journey, and for Merlin. It was the same trailer that would carry Merlin from the small farm in West Virginia to a grand farm in Kentucky, together with his beloved Tim. With family and friends gathered, all the young-ins patted Merlin, all the adults scratched his ears and nose, Grandma Mamie told him to keep his head out of people's windows, and finally, Grandpa Grant engulfed Merlin's head in his arms and cried for the love of a mule.

Never before had Quinn, a horseman through and through, seen anything like that mule, who was as gentle as a lamb and loved them all in return. Quinn now fully understood the bond between the man, Tim, and his mule, Merlin, and why they could not be separated while in this world.

Life for Tim and Merlin was beyond both of their expectations. Tim, under the guidance of great trainers, became one himself. And though he never trained a Churchill Down winner personally, he helped many who did. His long, fulfilling career of gentleness, love, and an incredible rapport with the horses was something that could not be matched by many.

Tim married a pretty, horse-loving Kentucky girl and had two horse-loving boys of his own, who were the apples of his eyes. And on a little 15-acre farm on the outskirts of Green Valley, Kentucky, Tim raised hay for a few horses and still enjoyed and loved the time with Merlin the mule. At the insistence of his boys, two orphaned 'jacks' were adopted, and much to his sons' delight, they were almost as intelligent and handsome as Merlin and pretty near as much fun as a day at the county fair. Merlin didn't extend a friendly hoof to the two rambunctious foals at first, but being a tolerant soul, they eventually won him with their unending braying for attention and the gentle nudging of their warm noses. Merlin decided they needed a shining example of what a mule should be, and with the same love and valiant protection he had for Tim, he soon claimed them as his own.

Merlin lived to be 37 years old and became loved by everyone from the mountains of West Virginia to the hills and meadows at Licking River Farm. In the corner of the farm, where champions who brought fame to themselves and to Licking River Farm rested in death, Merlin the Mule was laid among them. And though he never ran at the great tracks or won grand trophies, it seemed fitting to all that he join them, for he had the heart of a thoroughbred and surely the soul of a magician. Tim had an amazing life that sometimes he could hardly believe. He grew to love the Bluegrass State that he called home, but it could never replace his deep affection for West Virginia— and for those who raised him, supported him, and loved him till their dying days.

On one of his visits with the Sandy Creek family, and after a week of sweet days chasing his boys over the mountains, sharing stories, and showing them the old moonshiners' cabin once again, Tim sat down to eat with relatives under the giant old maple. Plates of fried chicken, potato salad, pole beans from the garden, freshly picked tomatoes, cornbread, and Aunt Celia's mouth-watering strawberry-rhubarb pie were passed around and enjoyed by all. When the week came to a close, Tim loaded the family into their station wagon. And among the farewell hugs, the waving hands, and the loving voices calling out goodbyes and *"Come back soon,"* Tim drove off.

Just as the car rolled down the gravel drive, he heard words that to this very day of storytelling is shared among the family, when a cousin shouted, "THERE GOES TIM JONES, WHO RODE A MULE AROUND THE WORLD!"

JESSE DEAN

What is done out of love always occurs beyond good and evil.

- Friedrich Nietzsche

1933

A mischievous and delightful boy, Jesse Dean Jackson was born in October 1933. From the moment he was laid in his mother's arms, he was a favorite of the whole Jackson family. With a head of curly blond hair, eyes the color of a crystal blue lake, a heart of gold, and a loyalty that could not be shaken, Jesse Dean was always one sin way from a meeting with the devil, but resting in the grace of God by his momma's prayers, he was also one deed away from a meeting with the Lord.

In a small country house with a front porch that set on a small knoll and treated to a view of a pebbled-filled little creek that flowed nearby, providing fun times for two growing boys and soft gurgling sounds for an afternoon nap in old wicker rockers, Jesse Dean's childhood in the mountains was good, simple, and uncomplicated. Owen and Elsa Jackson were the parents that many children would have envied. It was a dwelling of love, kindness, and hardworking parents who nurtured Jesse Dean and provided a home for him and his older brother, Rafe Aaron—filled with laughter, full bellies, the Bible, the rod of correction, and a deep belief in God. Sunday walks were made down the small dirt road to the Sunlight Baptist Church to hear the sacred words of their Savior preached, where Jesse Dean and Rafe were encouraged in the ways of faith, honesty, goodwill, and care of family.

But like the seasons in the hills that surrounded Sandy Creek, West Virginia, life was forever changing, and the desires for a future of goodness and happiness were to be tarnished and misplaced for a while. A labyrinthine of despair and sorrow would wind into the places of joy and trust to destroy lives but would fail in a way never expected.

September 1953

A war in a faraway country that was only studied in geography books brought letters to cousins, friends, and school classmates from the US Army, saying your draft number had been selected and to report to the nearest enlistment office. Though it was a 'peacetime draft,' it was nothing like the draft of WWII or later Vietnam. Rafe Aaron Jackson knew his number could be next, and though willing to fight for what he thought was a right and just cause, he also knew he did not want to be a foot soldier in a distant and unknown land.

On a cool fall morning, rising earlier than usual and telling Owen and Elsa they needed to meet some folks in town, 20-year-old Rafe, with an 18-year-old Jesse Dean tagging along, walked out of the dusty hollow to a neighbor's home, where they hitched a ride with Virgie Martin to Charleston, West Virginia.

On a sidewalk next to a tan stone building, Rafe stood for a few minutes, pondering his next course of action that would change his future, and then, without any hesitation, walked into the local Marine headquarters office. On that day in 1953, Rafe raised his hand in proud allegiance to his country and then, in a surprising scene from across the room, watched as Jesse Dean followed his big brother into the Marines with his own pledge of loyalty. Rafe felt a warm pride for his brother's courageous young heart but also a great concern as both brothers now faced an uncertain future and the telling of this day's events to their parents.

As they left the old stone building, they walked mostly in silence to the corner of Quarrier Street and climbed on a bus that would carry them toward home. They spoke nothing of the previous event, with both wondering in self mindfulness about the eventual outcome of today's actions, with bile churning in their stomachs but also a sense of peace and pride.

Walking into the home that raised them, their faces spoke of a need to engage in a discourse. When Elsa sensed such, she motioned for all to claim a front room chair. The conversation was terse and a surprise to Owen and a tearful Elsa, but there were no harsh words or no anger, just a produced period of a long silence.

Elsa spoke first, saying, "I need to do something in the kitchen," leaving a room of three men staring at their hands or the ceiling. She came back with a tray of pretty apple-blossom cups, strong coffee, fresh cream, and slices of a warm peach cobbler.

The stillness was broken by sips from well-used cups and compliments on her 'always perfect pies.' Rafe and Jesse Dean slowly shared the story that told of how both of their sons were now regulated to the United States Marines. An hour—and a few more tears—later, the sons of Owen and Elsa were engulfed in loving arms. They knew whatever the future held, they would always be encouraged and supported.

On a cold day in November of 1953, Jesse Dean and Rafe climbed on a Greyhound and, taking window seats, waved goodbye to a heavy-hearted but brave-faced Owen and Elsa. The boys themselves were filled with both angst and excitement at what lay ahead.

Fourteen hours later, in a small North Carolina town, the brothers walked off the bus and onto a place called Camp LeJeune and into a life that tested them for almost two long years.

The rigors of boot camp were easier on the Jackson brothers than on many others. Life in the West Virginia mountains was one of early mornings filled with farm work, long walks to a country school, hiking over hills hunting for game, chopping and gathering firewood, and rounding up the stray cow or pony that wondered off looking for that better clump of big bluestem. Country living had prepared them well for the basics of Marine training, but not for the Asian land of an enemy hoping to kill them. MOS testing for physical, mental, moral character, and responsibility was given. Both Jackson brothers, to their amazement, earned assignments to be Military Police and, in a matter of weeks, were assigned to a place hard to pronounce and even harder for them to maintain their sanity.

Landing at Camp Casey in Dongducheon, South Korea, with the 7th MP Company, Jesse Dean and Rafe weren't sure what to expect. But the friendly local native people, beautiful mountains, and breathtaking sunsets were not part of their expectations, and neither were the training and duties of an MP. The first two weeks, with 18-hour days, meant early to rise and early to bed, under the watchful eyes of a Master Sergent MP with a clipboard, a whistle, and a hip-mounted .45 APC

Colt pistol. He was their constant companion and instructor for the job that the brothers would soon be doing themselves.

At the 15-day mark, the brothers were 'cut loose' and armed with a .45 APC Colt 1911, a wooden baton, and red armbands stamped MP. It didn't take long to discover that an MP did more than arrest an inebriated Marine on a Friday night—it came with a demanding and startling mentality and a physical variety of duties.

Jesse Dean and Rafe found they, along with their MP brothers, were responsible for patrols in Camp Casey and the town of Dongducheon 24 hours a day, traffic control accident investigations, American vehicle/personnel checkpoints, general patrols, convoy escorts, special details such as protection and escorts for high ranking civilians and military personal, security for doctors and nurses who provided free medical treatments for orphans in nearby orphanages, working with local police, security searches of vehicles and checking VN civilian's ID's, manning observation posts in critical places such as hilltops, aid in setting up ambushes, handling a 'quick response force' as needed, and all the while covering a nine-mile area around the Tactical Area of Operations.

But the hardest tasks were of heart and mind, acting as a pastor, priest, counselor, and enforcer for the soldiers who struggled with long days and nights of homesickness, fear, loneliness, raging anger, and broken rules. Jesse Dean and Rafe's days were filled with a regimen that left time only for eating, latrine runs, a quickly written letter home, and nights filled with sweet dreams of the past and nightmares of the war.

A lot had been written about the mental and physical sides of wars. And for the Jackson brothers, the words foretold were true, as all the future years of their lives would be filled with crazy stories and funny jokes, midnight hours of tortured yells, and momentary wide-eyed looks of far-away places. But before those future years, Jesse Dean and Rafe, who lived the war daily, did the job they pledged to do and were asked to do without complaint. So, with laughter and anguish, through new friendships, through easy days of sending someone home to their family, and through the hard days of carrying someone to the medical tent who had attempted suicide, they did the job with strength and dignity.

But when November of 1955 rolled around after almost two years of military life, which consisted of pride and moments of insanity, the Jackson brothers, with grateful and gleeful hearts, bid friends, fellow soldiers, and South Korea goodbye. A C-124 Globemaster II lifted from the tarmac to transport the thankful Jackson brothers, along with many others, back to the United States, where a bus once more would carry them over the highways to their beautiful mountain home. However, this time, it brought them to be welcomed with a hand-painted banner, the biggest family gathering ever, and a future of bright hope and possibilities.

1956

Jesse Dean had been walking Gloria Faye Harris to church and to other local events for some time before his two-year side trip to Korea, and waiting for him in the cheerful gathering was a beautiful Gloria Faye, who, unknown to Jesse Dean, was greatly proud of him and loved him more than ever before. Seeing her again, Jesse Dean wondered if this petite, dark-haired, milk chocolate brown-eyed girl with a gentle and kind heart could still hold affection for him because he sure did for her.

On the ride back to the farm at Sandy Creek, they squeezed close together in the backseat of Owen's car. Gloria Faye took his hand in hers. Jesse Dean knew the fondness for him was still there, and his heart was about to burst with happiness!

Four months and a few days seem like forever when you are waiting for a day of happiness to arrive because the end of April of 1956 brought the families of Jesse Dean Jackson and Gloria Faye Harris, and friends and neighbors, to the little Sunlight Baptist Church at Sandy Creek for the wedding that was no surprise to anyone, except for Jesse Dean and Gloria Faye, who wondered if this day would really happen after all those years of hand-holding and church meetings.

Life for Jesse Dean and Gloria Faye didn't take long to settle into a pattern that was filled with dreams, laughter, and happiness. The first eleven months flew like a summer storm whirlwind. First, they rented a tiny white house on the outskirts of Charleston on Chandler Drive that provided a small garden patch. Then they purchased a used forest-green Chevy pickup that they had bought from Lincoln Jackson, Jesse Dean's favorite uncle and hunting buddy, then Gloria Faye worked a part-time job, which was perfect—for they hoped a little one would make an appearance in the near future. And lastly, Jesse Dean was offered an excellent position at Mountaineer Trucking that provided a good paycheck, medical insurance, and paid vacations. The future lay bright and wonderful before the young Jacksons.

Climbing into the cab of a 73' long tractor-trailer and shifting through 12 gears like a long-time pro, Jesse Dean delivered anything from farm tractors, steel beams, skits of food for animals and humans alike, and everything in between. It was a job that brought him pride and satisfaction. He was home for dinner every evening by 6 p.m., except when Gloria Faye was chopping, mixing, stirring, and whipping up eats as a part-time chef at the Creekside Café three days a week, where old and young waitresses alike delivered to waiting guests some of the best eats on the west end of

Charleston. Jesse Dean would park the old Chevy truck, and with Gloria Faye finishing up her shift, they would grab a back table and, while savoring the special on the menu, talk about their day and share local news and a piece of cake or pie to round off a hard-worked but gratifying day.

On the days Gloria Faye didn't work, she filled her hours with the chores of caring for her own home and walking the half-mile to Grandma Etta's small home on Ivy Drive to help with the care of Jesse Dean's 85-year-old grandmother, whom Gloria Faye loved as her own.

Grandma Etta's husband of 67 years, Alden Jackson, had been gone for a spell now, and as such, Grandma Etta enjoyed company almost as much as she loved her summer flower garden, buttermilk over warm cornbread in the winter, Sunday morning preaching, and her precious family of 12 children and umpteen grandchildren. But she especially loved Gloria Faye, who was now a part of Grandma Etta's family. She would sit for hours doing jigsaw puzzles with Grandma at an antique maple kitchen table covered with blue & white checkered oilcloth and let Grandma Etta beat her at the 'sinful' card game of gin rummy, as the preacher called it.

When one of Grandma's daughters arrived to take over Grandma Etta's care for a few hours in the evening, Gloria Faye would give Grandma a hug and kiss, toss on her coat, and head home to work on the starts of vegetable plants for the garden that would soon be put in the ground and to fix Jesse Dean dinner.

1957

It was a chilly, drizzly, overcast day in early March when the world of Jesse Dean and Gloria Faye came to a horrific halt, and life would be forever changed. At exactly 3:47 p.m. on a Tuesday afternoon, a familiar old Ford sedan slowed, a window rolled down, and someone asked a briskly walking Gloria Faye, "I'm headed your way. Want a ride home?"

Smiling at a neighbor of the Jackson family, Gloria Faye opened the door and said, "Thank you, Vernon Ray. I believe I do."

Shutting the car door and enjoying the brief warmth of the floor heater, Gloria Faye felt a sharpness, saw an engulfing blackness, and then there was nothing. Awaking, the pain was all she felt and all that she remembered. Not the ride, laying in the rain at the end of the sidewalk at her home, being lifted into Jesse's Dean's pickup, or being carried by Jesse Dean through the doors of Statt's Hospital. Nothing but a blank emptiness that made her head hurt and her body ache. She couldn't tell anyone anything of that day for Gloria Faye remembered absolutely nothing.

After X-rays that showed a hairline fracture and a small hematoma, doctors said her head injury was not severe but might be the cause of her selective memory loss, for she knew Jesse Dean and her family and lots of scattered memories.

In a world of unknown head trauma, Gloria Faye's lost consciousness might return in a few days, months, years, or maybe never, and only time would provide that answer. Gloria Faye spent nine days in a room filled with family, friends, and sympathetic faces. It didn't take long to learn what else had happened to Gloria Faye on that grim day, for a brutal rape would require emergency surgery, and it also didn't take long to realize that the tiny house would never be filled with children, for the savagery of that day removed that dream. Going home and supported by Jesse Dean's arms, Gloria Faye wept for herself and Jesse Dean and asked God for hope and comfort for the bitter disappointment that tore at their hearts.

Word spread of Gloria Faye's attack, and it filled the area surrounding Chandler Drive with fear, anger, and caution. Doors that were never locked were now locked, bolted windows were double-checked, baseball bats stood nearby for easy grabbing, and guns were loaded and placed in nightstands and kitchen drawers. Word of Gloria Faye's memory loss filled Vernon Ray Browne with a small sense of relief and safety.

The early weeks were filled with a fear in Vernon Ray's heart that Gloria Faye would remember, to the point that several times, Vernon Ray felt an urgent urge to load up his car and leave his home state behind him, telling no one where he was going, but he couldn't bring himself to do it. What about his heartbroken momma? Or his drinking buddies? All would wonder why he'd disappear without a cause or not telling them. So, Vernon Ray stayed in West Virginia, avoiding every event in Charleston or Sandy Creek that would have Gloria Faye in attendance and also laying low in the background wherever he did go. Feeling secure that the horrible transgression he did on that day in March seven months ago, when fueled by whiskey had caused a temporary loss of mind and control of his desires, would go undiscovered, Vernon Ray breathed in relief.

He was dead wrong.

On a warm, sunny November Saturday, tagging along with Jesse Dean to Lucenti's Auto Supply for some parts to get the old pick-up ready for winter, Gloria Faye was glancing through the truck's window, savoring the multi-colored trees and flowers of fall that lined the streets of Charleston, when a face she knew but had fearfully forgotten and was buried in an area of simmering pain, appeared briefly outside the door of Pile's Hardware Store. On that day, a sound oozed slowly from her throat into a harrowing scream that caused Jesse Dean to drive off the street, hitting the curb and taking Gloria Faye in his arms.

Unknown to Vernon Ray, that quick bop into town for some roofing nails was going to cost him more than he could ever imagine. Climbing back into his old sedan, along with a bottle of Jack Daniel's, Vernon Ray drove to Sandy Creek and up the Poca River Road to make the roof repairs on the old smokehouse for his momma.

After a time of comforting Gloria Faye, who sat motionless, quiet, and staring off as in a trance, Jesse Dean eased the truck back onto Washington Street, made a U-turn, and, driving slowly out of town, took in everything along the route they had just come on in hopes to see what could have produced his wife's reaction. But nothing seemed different from any other Saturday that he had run errands on.

In considerable concern, with his arm still around Gloria Faye, Jesse Dean decided to skip the auto parts store, and with as much speed as he could muster but without getting a ticket, he drove to the little white house and led her up the steps and through the door and to the kitchen table. As she sat there as if numb, Jesse Dean quietly heated water and poured it over a strainer, making a pot of tea—one of Gloria Faye's favorite afternoon respites.

Handing her a pretty cup with cabbage roses painted on the sides, Jesse Dean pulled up a chair next to her and, in a soft voice, said, "Gloria Faye, please, can you tell me what is wrong? What happened back there? And what can I do to help?"

Slowly picking up her cup with trembling hands and taking a small sip, Gloria Faye finally looked at Jesse Dean, and in a whisper filled with tears and anguish, she said, "Why did I get in the car? Why, oh why?!!!"

And with those words, Gloria Faye shared with her husband all of the horrible memories of that day that had come flooding back at the sight of the person who had almost destroyed them both—Vernon Ray Browne.

Jesse Dean and Gloria Faye spent the rest of the day until late into the evening in anger, tears, stop-and-go conversations, and forced bites of unwanted but needed food, wrapped in each other's arms for comfort in the little home that felt safe from the world.

Sunday dawned another warm fall day with a simple breakfast, a short drive to Parson's Chapel for worship, and a gentle refusal to Sunday dinner at the preacher's house, because the day was already exhausting for them. Jesse Dean and Gloria Faye drove home with hymns from WCHS coming from the radio, taking some small comfort from the words of the songs.

After partaking of cheese and pickle sandwiches, Gloria Faye said, "I'm awfully tired, Jesse Dean, and I need to lay down for a while."

Jesse Dean replied, "Good idea. Try to get a nap, and I'll run out to my mom and dad's, drop off the tools I borrowed last week, visit with them for a bit, and maybe quiet my thoughts. See you soon, beautiful."

Hugging each other for a few seconds, they both headed in different directions. Both knew there would probably be no rest for Gloria Jean, no quieting for Jesse Dean's mind, and no thought of what the next three hours would hold.

At the home of Owen and Elsa, Jesse Dean found his dearest Grandma Etta sitting in a kitchen rocker with his father at the table, where they chatted and rested after a hearty Sunday dinner.

"Where's Mom?" Jesse Dean asked.

He was told she had walked up to Robert and Bess Hackney's to deliver food—for illness had hit the home—and sit with the Hackneys a while and commiserate on the weather and the sicknesses going around. With an odd expression, Jesse Dean sat at the table for a few minutes, jumping up and pacing the kitchen as if waiting for a new baby to arrive.

Owen and his mother, Etta, exchanged looks, knowing something was on Jesse Dean's mind. But when he spoke, what he said shocked them to the core of their souls, and Etta said in a hushed tone, "Oh, dear Lord, let this not be true."

His story started out that it was just a straight drive to Owen and Elsa's, a 35-minute run from Charleston to Sandy Creek, but the old drive along the Poca River Road provided time for Jesse Dean to be alone with the incredible information about the last days whirling in his mind. So, when he got to the turn-off to the Browne farm, he told himself he only wanted to speak to Vernon Ray, to ask him why he did what he did, and to look for regret and repentance in his eyes.

Pulling into a little country store that was set at the intersection of the two roads, Jesse Dean walked in, bought a bottle of Coke and a pack of Pall Mall's, chatted briefly with the teenager working that Sunday afternoon, and sat on the old bench out front of the store to calm his nerves and ponder on what he should do. Getting into his truck, Jesse Dean drove a mile down the road and, with no one in sight, he parked his truck behind an old stand of Eastern Red cedars and walked into the woods that would lead him to the home of Mary Browne.

With his mind spinning and his heart thumping, he kept asking himself, "What am I doing here?" and then, he would tell himself, "For Gloria Faye; this is for Gloria Faye!"

Coming upon the small farm, Jesse Dean saw Vernon Ray before Vernon Ray saw him. With an arm full of shingles and ready to climb a ladder,

Jesse Dean moved quietly closer and said in a low voice, "Hello, Vernon Ray. I think we need to talk."

He saw no flashes of regret or repentance in Vernon Ray's, only a moment of fear and panic that quickly gave way to a cold, hard stare, and that was when Jesse Dean knew why he had come to avenge his wife, and so did Vernon Ray.

The lunge by Vernon Ray toward the corner of the smokehouse was futile, for Jesse Dean was on Vernon Ray in the blink of an eye, and though they were pretty well matched in size, the anger and adrenaline made Jesse Dean have the rage and strength of a red-flagged bull. Grabbing Vernon Ray, Jesse Dean began fighting like a madman, landing the first punch. Jesse Dean picked up an old heavy hammer and slammed Vernon Ray to the ground with a powerful blow to the head.

Breathing hard and standing over the motionless body, he told Vernon Ray, "Get up! Get up, you worthless coward. Get up!" Jesse Dean looked into Vernon Ray's eyes, and knowing what death looked like from the days of war, he knew that Vernon Ray had lost his battle and would never hurt another woman again.

Leaning back against the smokehouse, Jesse Dean's mind and gut twirled and twisted as if a maddening disease was overtaking him and filled with what had just happened and what the outcome would be. Though he didn't come to kill Vernon Ray, the law might think otherwise after learning the real reason he came to the house on Higginbottom Road. With one more look at Vernon Ray and muttering a distraught prayer for the sin he had just committed, Jesse Dean stood still, staring off, and then knew what he had to do.

Looking around and not seeing or hearing anyone, Jesse Dean heaved Vernon Ray onto his shoulder, picked up the hammer, and, along with the weight of the world on his back, quietly walked with a stumbling pace around the base of the mountain till he was out of sight of Henry and Mary Browne's farm, and then with one more draw of unknown strength, Jesse Dean headed up the mountain to a flat top where he and Vernon Ray's body both collapsed onto the field of soft fall wheat. Knowing he couldn't carry him any longer, he took Vernon Ray's belt, wrapping it around his ankles, and began to drag Vernon Ray through the half-mile-long meadow and up over a small incline to finally let the body rest at the edge that overlooked the home of Owen and Elsa Jackson. And it was there he left Vernon Ray, running down to the farmhouse below and tossing the hammer into an old dried-up cistern, and entered into the kitchen where Owen and Grandma Etta sit and the tale of brutal revenge for Gloria Faye was told.

The first reactions were quiet, with wide-eyed looks of disbelief. Then, with Owen rushing to the backdoor and looking upward to the hilltop as if he could see the body, he said, "Son, we got to call the sheriff."

Jesse Dean sat with his head in his hands among soft groans of regret, but it was Grandma Etta who remained like a stone and said nothing.

After what seemed like an eternity, Grandma Etta finally spoke in a low and even voice, "Jesse Dean, what you have done is against God's laws, and it was a vile thing to do, and I have to say that my heart is surely broken by this deed. But I understand why you did it, for what that Satan-filled man did to Gloria Faye. So, today, we will do something the Jacksons have never done before. And no, Owen, we aren't calling the sheriff; we are going to give Jesse Dean and Gloria Faye another chance at life, for they deserve it."

Owen started to speak, but after a look at his mother's face, he knew it would be useless, and Owen once more knew he would listen and obey the woman with great wisdom who raised him, and so he said no more. Sitting quietly once more but only briefly, Grandma Etta began to sway in the old oak rocker as Owen stared out the back window and Jesse Dean walked the floor.

Breaking the silence, Grandma Etta said, "I know what must be done and where to do it. Owen and Jesse Dean, we must be strong of body and strong of mind, and we must swear this day to never mention what took place to no one but only to God in prayers for repentance and forgiveness."

With nods of heads and soft "I swear," Grandma Etta lay before them her thoughts, and so the vanishing of Vernon Ray began. Climbing the mountain was strenuous, and Grandma Etta, an aged 85-year-old, could not make the climb, so Owen knelt and Jesse Dean lifted the 5' feet and 112-pound woman onto Owen's back, and they continued to where Vernon Ray lay, as if asleep. Lifting Granny Etta back to the ground, the three stood with vacant stares at the body of a man they had known for a lifetime. Without speaking, they began the not-too-distant walk to the other side of a low hill, dragging the body of a country boy along with their troubled hearts.

They crossed the hilltop meadow and then carried Grandma Etta once more but down the short hill to an area that Grandma Etta knew well, where white pines and mountain laurel grew, and colorful leaves from the maple saplings had fallen. They lowered her to the ground, and she began to guide her son and grandson. Knowing what to look for but not sure exactly where, Jesse Dean and Owen scowled the area to finally see past some fallen rocks and on through wild ferns and low evergreen branches to a hole in the hill that led to the old abandoned mine. The mine was cold, dark, and damp and smelled of mildew and rotten eggs, with only the dulled glow of their flashlights to see the dry floor and reflections off the wet walls. Going deeper into the dim darkness, they found small mounds of coal tossed to the side here and there, and behind one of them, they lifted and laid the last earthly remains of Vernon Ray Browne.

With ambivalent hearts, they walked away and never looked back.

Weary and broken in soul, Jesse Dean, Owen, and Grandma Etta slowly retraced the trail up the low mountain, across the hilltop field, and down to the Jackson home. In exhaustion and cold, they settled in the kitchen once more and said not a word, with only the sound of the mantle clock that ticked the time and life away.

Jesse Dean finally spoke and, in tears and with hands clasped together, asked God, Owen, and Grandma Etta for forgiveness. Walking to the back door, he was greeted by Elsa returning home. He said to her, "Sorry I can't stay, Mom. I've been too long already, and I need to get home to Gloria Faye." He hugged Elsa goodbye, and she watched him walk to the pickup with a confusing sense of change in her Jesse Dean.

It was a full week before Mary Browne decided something might be wrong. Vernon Ray wandered off frequently for a few days at a time, but three days was the longest. She had lost her husband many years before, and Vernon Ray was her only child. Though he disappointed her in many ways, he was still a comfort, and for this, she was worried.

Walking a mile to use a neighbor's phone, she made her first call to share her unsettled thoughts. It was a few more days before the Charleston Daily Mail reported that the mother of Vernon Ray

Browne was concerned enough to call the Sandy Creek Sheriff's Department and the Kanawha County Police to voice her worries.

But it took only three minutes of reading for Gloria Faye to know Vernon Ray would never be found and that on a Sunday afternoon a week ago, as she lay on her bed questioning God about the future, her husband Jesse Dean had probably decided it for them.

Jesse Dean had said almost nothing upon his return from Owen and Elsa's other than, "I'm just tuckered out, Gloria Faye. I think I'll take it easy the rest of the day." Heating up some leftover soup for them both, Jesse Dean sat quietly in his favorite chair, watching the little television they had saved for, and later slipped gently into bed next to Gloria Faye, and both slept a troubled sleep.

The area of the Browne farm was searched high and low, as was the hillside behind the house, but no sign or smell that even the scent dogs could detect was found. In the end, it was decided, much to Mary Browne's tears of dismay and disbelief, that Vernon Ray Browne had gotten serious about leaving West Virginia and had made off to places unknown. His friends felt this was probably the case, but Mary Browne didn't, and in her heart, knew something terribly wrong had happened. It was something that her heart would prove to be true in July 1961.

July 1961

Haunting of the past happened on a night in July 1961 when the earth around Charleston, West Virginia, was as saturated as a trillion water-logged sponges. On that night, when the mountains and the soil on them could hold no more, the doors to a long-remembered nightmare of 1957 opened wide. In the blackness of night and pouring rain, with no one watching, it started near the top of a mountain below the old McFarland Cemetery, where the land heaved almost with a sigh and began a slow move that carried along with it slender pines, old trees of maple, oak, and beech, scent filled magnolias, shrubs, tall grasses, rocks large and small, and coffee brown thick mud. It moved over the sloping terrain without hesitation, and now, at least 30 ft. wide and 2 ft. tall, it pushed across Sugar Creek Drive, taking everything in its path with it. It gained speed as it widened to 40 ft. wide and 3 ft. tall, crossing the rugged area, and aimed the river of mud toward Chandler Drive. Unknown to most of Charleston who were nestled in their homes or those who had fled the rising Elk River earlier in the day to shelters, the worst was yet to come. For lingering in the moonless darkness of rain and thunder was a monster waiting to show its destructive power to use the growing mass for great misery and sorrow.

At the little white house of Jesse Dean and Gloria Faye was a nervous Jesse Dean, for the days of rain had caused the small creek that ran in front of their home and the length of Chandler Drive to swell from barely a trickle of inches to at least 3 feet and still rising. With his help, he and Gloria Faye had earlier filled several suitcases with clothes for the family of four, a wicker basket with food and drinks, and a small satchel of toys and light jackets, all of which were set by the back door.

Also with them that night was Grandma Etta, who they had talked into staying with them due to the weather, and Jesse Dean's cousin, Marshall Allen, another of Grandma's grandsons, who was visiting while home from West Virginia University for the summer. It had been a pleasant couple of days having Marshall Allen 'Marsh' with them, sharing old family tales, helping in the kitchen, playing with the little ones, evening games of gin rummy, and watching Dennis the Menace, Wagon Train, Hazel, and Lassie on the little TV.

At 9:20 p.m., a clap of deafening thunder shook the little house, waking the babies and causing Jesse Dean to jump to his feet and rush to the front door and out onto the porch. What Jesse Dean saw made his heart leap in his chest, and a gasp came from his throat. For the little creek was now lapping at the second step to the porch, and he knew soon the racing water would probably come higher even to cross the threshold. Running back into the house and standing still briefly, Jesse Dean said in a rush of breath and concern, "We have to get out of the house before the water overtakes us. Gloria Faye, get the babies; Marsh, grab the suitcases; Grandma, grab the satchel, and everyone, head to the back door!"

It surprised and relieved Jesse Dean how quickly everyone reacted, without a comment to Jesse Dean's shout of orders. Making their way out of the house and across the back yard to a raised concrete patio, there sat, elevated up and against the hillside behind the house, a small shed, and it was there they were headed to.

With another crack of thunder followed by bolts of lightning, everyone could see the creek water rushing toward them. Jesse Dean yelled over the sound of water, wind, and rain, "Throw the stuff on the shed and head for the hill!"

Fighting against nature and fear, they did as Jesse Dean said and began the ascent of the slippery, slushy slope. Marsh grabbed a clinging Cathy, Gloria Faye wrapped Joe-Joe tight in her arm, and Grandma Etta, trying her best but slipping back toward the muddy water below her, was heaved onto Jesse Dean's back, as his father did some years ago. The Jacksons begin the climb of their lives. Crawling the rain-soaked incline and grasping at small shrubs, sagging tree branches, and an occasional rock, the family edged upward in a physical fight with a 90-foot hill. Over the blowing rain, the roar grew, and a brilliant white lightening that seemed to light the entire world caused both Jesse Dean and Grandma Etta to turn toward the sound. Revealed coming toward them was a wall of churning and rolling debris, filled with mud that, for a few minutes, gave a black gaping scene like the opening entrance to the tomb where Vernon Ray Browne lay in death.

Jesse Dean shouted, "Hang on, Granny!"

Grandma Etta screamed, "No, no, no!" She shut her eyes and clung even greater to her grandson, for she was sure they were going to be swallowed and punished for that long-ago sin. But this black night was not their time to die, and along with the others, they seized and clutched and clawed up the hill, where, to their amazement, were neighbors with flashlights and outcast hands standing in the tortuous rains and who pulled them to safety and into their homes. Though soaked, cold, and shivering, Grandma Etta fell to her knees as did everyone else, praising God for his saving care.

Huddled the next morning around the radio and TV, as they, along with their neighbors, sat and ate gratefully what was before them, did they learn of the destruction and death that had awaited others. For, on the night of July 19th, two monster flash floods started on a mountain slope and, with the eagerness of a leopard in a chase, fed the river of mud. In its path, it ravaged down the hillsides into the hollows of Garrison Avenue and Chandler Drive, taking with it homes and lives. In the dark of night, 33 souls would die, changing forever the lives of families, where thousands would be left homeless, and millions of dollars of damage and loss. It would prove to be the worst flood in history in Kanawha County and also bring to the hearts of Jesse Dean and Grandma Etta a cold sorrow of the past and deliver to Mary Browne a bitterly answered prayer.

October 1961

In a quiet and lonely corner of a densely wooded West Virginia mountain lay the remains of a skeleton. No one had ventured near the hidden crevice, devoid of light. It had once been an opening to a desolate and worked-out mine many years ago. He would leave his mortality behind and lay there through the bitter winters, warm springs, hot summers, and crisp falls, all of which he would never have a part of again. There wouldn't be much left of his physical life, and even that would have eventually disappeared if not for a rambunctious, small, black, white, and tan beagle.

But that July, after nine days of tumultuous rains, the likes that hadn't been seen in decades, where the skies opened wide as if it was the coming of the Lord, rained a deluge upon the whole of Kanawha County, and began to move rock and soil and whole mountainsides, opening up places that laid uncovered and not remembered for years, and where a long-forgotten mine would give up its secret. An overcast day with only the faintest of daylight trying to beckon its way through moving shadows of clouds, a yawning hole in the side of a short mountain, where stunted red and white pines grew, and a few mountain laurels were still in bloom, would give up its hiding place after days of beating rain had washed the soil away with tiny rivulets of water.

A decaying scent found its way from the decades-old mine to the sharp nose of Braxton, old man Clendenin's new beloved puppy. Ignoring the calls of his master but not the beckoning of a new, wonderful smell, Braxton plunged into the mine, following a dark shaft. Being led by two dark brown ground-hugging orifices and years of breeding that triggered a desire to hunt down a scent, whatever it was or wherever it be, Braxton was in doggy heaven and most pleased at what he had found. What seemed like an eternity of calling the pup, and much to old man Clendenin's great relief, Braxton immerged with muddy paws, a muddy nose, and a dirty, rotted rag that turned out to be what was left of a shirt of a man long gone but not forgotten. The mystery of a missing man was about to be solved, but the *when, why*, and *how* would go forever unanswered. But for now, Braxton, the beagle, got a gentle rub between two soft, floppy ears, and he walked proudly next to the old man who loved him dearly.

May 1962

The five years that followed the recovery of Gloria Faye's memories was measured in steps for her and Jesse Dean. And the nightmares of a flood that would change lives forever, would bring broken bits and pieces for the Jackson's, and for the city of Charleston. Life though filled with its bittersweet moments had to be lived, and Jesse Dean, Gloria Faye, Owen and Grandma Etta had to learn to live with past pain, hidden secrets, to close old wounds, and to open their hearts and souls to the future days that was given anew to each of them of bright skies, flower gardens, picnics, birthdays, and games of gin rummy.

But the grandest day of all was the adoption of Catherine Faye, who would bring the patter of sweet little feet to Jesse Dean and Gloria Faye's home, of an unmeasurable amount of joy. Baby showers were planned and filled with gifts of all kinds, to welcome "Cathy" to a home of love and a wonderous family who would read her stories from the family Bible and guard her through life. The future would hold another blessing for Jesse Dean and Gloria Faye, where a year later the adoption of a chubby delightful baby boy who would be named Joseph Owen or "Joe-Joe" as Cathy childish chatter called him, and who many would remark that he had the mischievous look of his daddy, much to Jesse Dean's delight.

Though cleaned, repaired, and restored, they left the little house on the westside of Charleston and bought a salmon-colored brick ranch that set nowhere near water and on a raised knoll, in the nearby town of Cross Lanes. The years that Jesse Dean and Gloria Faye shared there raising Cathy and Joe in a home filled with the flow of family and friends, was never taken for granted, with time passing as the swiftness of an archer's arrow.

Along with that flight of life, came the deaths of Grandma Etta, Owen and Elsa, Gloria Faye's parents, and many other family and friends. Their beloved Cathy and Joe made everyone proud over the years, and eventually made Jesse Dean and Gloria Faye grandparents five times over.

Sometimes and without cause, Jesse Dean and Gloria Faye would remember the past in quiet, somber thoughts, giving thanks to God for the forgiveness of those harrowing days of yesteryears, and where those times would often lead them to climb into Jesse Dean's Chevy Blazer for a drive, and time of reflection.

In the Spring Hill cemetery, not far from a tall obelisk of an old Kanawha County founding family, lay the remains of Mary Browne's son. On a gray marble headstone of a square cut top, and plain in design, were the words that read;

VERNON RAY BROWNE

B: April 13th 1937

D: 1961?

LOST IN LIFE – FOUND IN DEATH

PLACED IN A TOMB BY HANDS KNOWN ONLY
TO GOD.

If anyone was watching, there, on a raised incline among old trees, stood a couple staring off over the cemetery, with heads bowed in silence for a brief time and with clasped hands. Then walking away as if in deep sorrow. Jesse Dean and Gloria Faye never forgot the grievous deed done to Gloria Faye or the egregious deed done by Jesse Dean. No amount of time could ever erase those remembrances.

A life together that started out with great angst and sorrow now ended with years of joy and peace. In old age, Jesse Dean and Gloria Faye would be laid in the mountain soil near Sandy Creek, West Virginia, where tall winter grasses blew and summer wildflowers bloomed.

DELLA, JOSIE, AND LEAH

I shall be telling this with a sigh
Somewhere ages and ages hence:
Two roads diverged in a wood, and I—
I took the one less traveled by,
And that has made all the difference.

- Robert Frost

1936

In the little town of Sandy Creek, West Virginia, in a back bedroom of her parents' home on Little Sandy Fork, Geraldine Jackson paced from wall to wall with the occasional pause by the tall oak bedpost to steady herself when a contraction took hold and almost brought her on her knees. And it was where she cussed under her breath to the man who told her he was unable to produce any progeny and that their times together would produce nothing but enjoyment.

Geraldine now knew those encounters in the barn hay-lined loft or in the back seat of his two-door sedan would produce more than just an hour of enjoyment, for each stabbing pain reminded her of what it was. She also now knew Ferrill James was a lying bastard who was healthy in every way, and the child pushing its way into the world would be a bastard, too, and viewed with disdain by the world. The hours seemed to pass slower than the pace of a river snail when finally, with Geraldine's mother's guiding hands, she laid back on the spring bed of her youth, knowing that an event was about to happen that would change everything.

In between flashes of discomfort and agony, Geraldine thought how she imagined what was happening today would only happen with a solid marriage under her feet and a husband by her side. But alas, that was not to be, and on a chilly and overcast morning at 11:18 a.m. in March of 1936, Geraldine Jackson brought forth a girl child she named Della James.

In a cheery yellow room in the maternity ward at the St. Frances Hospital in Charleston, West Virginia, Susanna Jackson Lane gripped the marble sill of a large window that overlooked a small garden filled with spring daffodils and multi-colored tulips as she stood while waiting for the next spasm to take hold of her body.

As with most expectant women at the end of a nine-month journey of change, she wasn't just pleased that her time had come to have her first child, but she was elated and would have jumped for joy if she could have—because from the beginning, the pregnancy, it had been one of months of morning sickness, constant back pain, water weight gain, and swollen feet that were agony to walk on. So far, though, the labor was going fast and not nearly as painful as she had seen her sisters and friends experience.

The nuns who ran the hospital and were top-notch nurses, said it wouldn't be long now, and so Susanna was mighty relieved, and the sunshine and pretty flowers made her smile. But for reasons unknown at the time, Susanna felt something 'pop' in her stomach, and a searing pain sent her to the black and white speckled floor tile, where she cried out. As hands carried her to her bed, a needle was inserted in her arm, and a small mask was placed on her face. As she drifted off, all Susanna could think of was the precious babe she hoped to hold and the regrets of her complaining.

In an operating room with rushed doctors and staff, a small bundle was lifted from Susanna's womb at 2:20 p.m. and wrapped in a warm blanket. Viewing a scene that no doctor wants to see, a surgeon removed Susanna's damaged uterus that would never carry another child. Sometime later, on that flower-scented and sunny spring day in April 1936, they laid a healthy baby in Susanna's arms, a girl child whom she would name Josie Lane.

The midwife was a small black woman with swept-back gray hair in a bun who was considered the 'best of the best' among mid-wives in the east end of Charleston, West Virginia. With a friendly face lined with middle-aged wrinkles, a kind smile, and a gentle voice, Sylvia Fisher brought great comfort and great care to the woman under her watchful eyes. In her small white house, which was sparkling clean with painted walls of pale green, was a bedroom where Sylvia helped to bring 'her babies,' as she called them, into the world.

On that warm day, sitting on an old hickory birthing stool, was Miriam Jackson Rowe, straining with closed eyes and clenched fists for what she hoped would soon be the end of a way-to-painful and long delivery.

On the front porch sat Miriam's husband, Sheldon, along with Sylvia's husband, who was home from work. Mr. Fisher knew the part he occasionally played in holding distracting conversations with soon-to-be fathers. Miriam could hear faint voices from the porch, but between her groans, along with Sylvia's soft words of encouragement and the gentle singing of her mother and two sisters who had settled in the corner of the room, Miriam rose from the chair and walked to the bathroom and back, told Sylvia something new was happening with an urge that wasn't there before. Sylvia lined the birthing chair with clean, soft towels, as a slightly bent over and grimacing Miriam returned to the chair and, with everyone speaking gentle words of encouragement, pushed with all the strength her tired body could muster. Quicker than she could have imaged, she delivered into the hands of the midwife at 7:40 p.m. in May of 1936 a girl child she would name Leah Rowe.

The three sisters were thrilled at the births of their daughters—even Geraldine, as she knew her illegitimate child would be swaddled in love and care as much as the legitimate ones would be.

A week later, grandparents, aunts, uncles, and cousins of all ages stood in awe at the three small specimens of babes with tiny tuffs of light hair and various colors of blue eyes that lay nestled together on Grandpa and Grandma Jackson's big feather bed in the sleep of innocence. Little did everyone know how those tiny souls would grow to be like sisters and how life would bring both similarities and differences to their lives. With all the normal growth events taking place from crawling to walking in the first two years, the sight of the three tiny girls holding hands and toddling across a grassy yard was a sweet sight to behold.

By the age of two years, the 'triplets,' as they were now referred to, were bonded in a way that would last a lifetime, though life itself would find their paths diverged. With homes in and around the town of Charleston, West Virginia, the triplets spent hours and days playing together first on thick blankets on the floor with small gumming toys craved by Great-Grandpa Grant of beech wood that soothed tiny gums, to a hand-made playpen that cousin Waldon pieced together from small willow tree branches, after seeing a 'baby cage' in a magazine at the barber shop in Sandy Creek. Filled with homemade dolls, stuffed bears, metal rattles that twirled, and the occasional soft cookie, they played for hours, jabbering to each other in a language no one understood but them.

By the age of three, the triplets had lost almost all of the babyish similarities of the first year of flaxen-colored hair and blue eyes. With their parent's DNA coming forth, changes brought out three different appearances but with a few family traits remaining, such as the Jackson nose and a tiny dimple in only one cheek. Della was a beauty of medium height and medium size with hair the color of milk chocolate and deep blue eyes that would take on black specks. Della was pretty as a picture, the most talkative, with a sweet smile and bubbly personality, but would later show a sad and troubled soul. Josie was a big-boned and tall girl with inherited traits from her large daddy. With hair that had turned to soft black and dark eyes that now held only splinters of blue, she had the beauty of a gypsy charmer. But the charm would change and bring on woes for many in years to come. Leah, the youngest of the three, was a delight to all. Of medium height with a tad of chubbiness that would change into a shapely beauty, Leah would be called the fair maiden of the three, and she was that in more ways than appearance. Leah's hair remained flaxen in color, eyes of now soft green with only a hint of a blue ring, a sunshine smile, and gentle nature. She would be a favorite, whose life would be full of joy and deep sorrow.

By the age of four years, more differences in the three became apparent to all who shared their world, and those differences made each one unique, while many shared traits still remained within. Personalities came forth with Della, the first to be born, being the leader of their many activities and adventures. Josie, the second born, was a follower but whose silliness and fun caused much-invented mischievousness of the three. Leah, the third born, was a reserved and keen watcher but participated in all of the triplets' antics with good-hearted fun. The three never tired of each other with days of play and nights of giggles, which were constantly at hand, and they loved each other dearly from the very first.

By the age of six, the triplets were first graders in different schools, and though not together as often, joyful and sweet times were still shared. Where many Saturdays were spent together in the winter, sledding down Dunker's Hill—so named because you could end up in the shallow cold creek if your boot-covered feet failed you—or swinging on an innertube and dropping in the warm Pocatalico River on a hot summer day. And where many Sundays were spent in the little Sunlight Baptist Church, singing old hymns that they didn't totally understand (was a sweet chariot really going to swing low and get them?) and listening to the 'fire, hell, and brimstone' preachers that they watched in wide-eye wonder (and later said bedtime prayers that they might be saved from brimstone if they ate all of their vegetables?). Of which, both days were followed by supper at Grandpa and Grandma Jackson's house.

Be it any day, gathered around a table filled with big bowls of wonderful food in a warm, cozy kitchen with the chattering of loved ones and softly falling snow, or a pot-luck dinner under a shade tree from the blazing sun and chasing each other in the almost dry creek-bed that ran nearby, these days were favorite times that would carry them through life with precious memories. But it was about this age that the triplets began to discover something that was to bring them gaggles of laughter and eventually lead to a solemn awakening.

For in the summer of 1942, the discovery in the area of trickery or practical jokes first took hold in their young minds, as the triplets played one of many future and secretive pranks. On this hot Saturday, while many family members were at Grandpa and Grandma Jackson's house, a group of older cousins decided to cool off by going swimming, and not wanting to take the triplets along because they would need to be closely supervised—and not wanting to take on that responsibility for the day—left them behind. This not only hurt Della, Josie, and Leah's feelings but also made them angry.

Pretending to go play with the new litter of piglets in the barn, and with a thought of revenge forming, the triplets grabbed an empty seed sack hanging on the barn wall and, unbeknown to anyone, followed the cousins to the little Pocatalico River, which ran from a branch off of Sandy Creek and flowed through the town of the same name.

With the older cousins yelling and busy holding swim contests, swinging off of a rope hanging from an oak branch dropping into the river, and dunking each other to a fare-thee-well, the triplets, well hidden from sight and, silent as could be, sneaked to the spot where all the shoes and socks were hidden and placed them into the old seed sack. Taking the sack, the triplets walked a path through the woods back to the Jackson house so as not to be seen and tossed the sack along the path, where it was sure to be found.

After several hours of water adventures and good fun, the older cousins climbed out of the creek, dried off, and began looking for shoes and socks that were nowhere to be found. Confusion and head-scratching reigned, followed by angry complaining on the painful walk back to the

Jackson farm on a sharp gravel and rocky road. Arriving at their grandparent's home, they told of their shoes disappearing, and with old spare shoes from a bedroom closet, the older cousins, along with parents, aunts, and uncles, went back to the river to search for the missing items. This time, Della, Josie, and Leah were allowed to follow and, pretending to help, suggested the path through the woods, where, sure enough, the shoes were found. Questions and comments were discussed on the walk back to the house, with all kinds of thoughts being thrown out, but no one noticed the three snickering little girls at the end of the group, who knew then what the delights of pranks could await them.

During the next eleven seasons of life, years as the triplets grew into womanhood, so did the pranks. They were always amazed that through the years, no one ever suspected them of the odd or weird events that took place, beginning with the disappearing shoe prank. The day the family cow walked into Grandma Etta Jackson's kitchen and began to snack on a bunch of carrots, much to Grandma's annoyed surprise. The day the entire flock of chickens had escaped the chicken yard to be found on the road by the Jackson farmhouse, scratching among the dust and gravel, needing half a day to round them up. The day Mr. Pauley's sweet old bull was caught in the garden, gorging it's self on carrots, corn, tunips and peas, and had to be led back home by an annoyed Grandpa Alden, who missed the devoured sweet corn that was planned for supper. The day a garden snake was found in the Sunday school teacher's desk drawer, and her screams could be heard for a country mile. The day when a pretty box turtle crawled out from under a pillow when Uncle Owen went to bed one night, causing a stir-up between him and his brother, Orion, as Owen was sure he had put it there. The day that Mrs. Melton's pies, which were cooling on a kitchen window sill, disappeared only to be found resting on a front porch banister. The day when great Aunt Leota's water stopped working, and after hours of looking for the cause, it was discovered that the exterior main water valve had been turned off. The day a raccoon had been locked in the little Sunlight Baptist Church on a Saturday morning, so when Miss Lilly came to clean later that day for Sunday services, she was as surprised at seeing the raccoon as it was at seeing her, with both running toward the open door. The day when fishing poles had been left by the back door to be used later in the day but were no longer there, only to be found hanging from the branches of a small willow tree on the hillside.

These pranks and many others continued until the triplets' senior year in high school, when their most adventurous trickery was to end the years of great fun and laughter that had done no harm to anyone.

Until now in the summer of 1952.

On that hot Saturday night at about 1 p.m., and previously deciding to expand their area of pranking, when everyone was in the beds at Grandpa and Grandma Jackson's house, supposedly sleeping soundly for early Sunday services, the triplets slipped quietly out of a window and, with flashlights from the barn that was hidden earlier, made their way by a sliver of a cloudy moon down the mile-long dusty road to the little country store for the best prank ever.

Creeping close to the little store, by the name of The Poca Pantry, and checking the windows, they found one open, and removing the window screen, they climbed inside quiet as a shadow. Each claiming a side of the store, the triplets glided along shelf by shelf, switching items around and moving other items higher up or lower down. Whispering and giggling in low voices, they wished they could have been there when the store opened up on Sunday afternoon to see the looks on Mr. & Mrs. Corbett's faces.

But unbeknown to the triplets, Elmer Corbett, the owner, had heard the movements below as he and his wife, Edna, had taken to sleeping Saturday nights at the little store due to a break-in a few weeks back. As quietly as a mouse, Mr. Corbett moved barefoot and slow down the back stairs in the store, and with a gun in hand, made his way toward the front of the store, only to stumble and fall over a mop and bucket that Mrs. Corbett had forgotten to put away. He cried out in alarm and pain.

The noise froze the triplets in place for a few seconds when, finally, Josie ran for the front door and, in a loud whisper, told the others to run, too! Following Josie, the triplets took off across the small parking area and headed into the thick woods that would take them back to the road to home to make their escape until a gunshot was heard from behind them.

Luckily, Mr. Corbett wasn't a great shot, especially in the dark of night, but even still, a bullet hit home. Yelping in pain and dropping to the ground, Leah was holding her leg and bleeding. Grabbing her up under her arms and wrapping them around their shoulders, Della and Josie swiftly began dragging her by her good leg, disappearing into the night and woods, making a slow but successful progress to the Jackson farmhouse. Climbing steps to the front porch, the triplets were heard by Grandma, who opened the door to three terrified girls, with one bleeding.

Though Grandpa Alden was a veterinarian, he knew how to handle many human illnesses and accidents, and so without a word, he moved Leah to his small office on the side of the house, where she was laid on a table. By now, the entire household was awake and watching the event, all with very concerned and curious faces, wondering if Leah would be alright and how she came to be out and about and shot. Grandpa Alden, with the aid of Grandma Etta, gently examined the wound and, seeing that it wasn't serious and only a flesh wound, began to wash it and apply an antiseptic. After wrapping Leah's leg with a clean bandage and filled with relief that no one was seriously hurt, the three girls were taken into the kitchen and seated at the kitchen table.

There, their 6'3" grandfather stared at them in a compilating silence of worry and outrage. "What happened tonight and why? And leave no telling of the story untold."

Grandpa Alden then listened to the tale of mischief.

For the first time in their entire lives, a fear of this beloved man took hold, for they knew their high jinks had gone wrong and could have had horrible consequences. Towering over them at the end of the table and surrounded by Grandma Etta, along with a visiting uncle, aunt, and many cousins, Grandpa Alden waited in stony silence.

When Leah began to weep, not only in fear but pain also, the story came tumbling out like a mountain waterfall and cascaded into the telling of many past events. Eyes downcast, Della sat without moving except for the growing rage on her face of betrayal. Josie threw her head back and wailed, blaming Della and Leah for all of their past adventures. And Leah, now somewhat recovered, stared at Della and Josie with a tear-stained face in disappointment that neither cousin came to her defense.

Grandpa Alden raised his hand, and the room finally stilled with a tense quietness. Grandpa said, "The events of this night are never to be spoken about by anyone or to anyone outside of this house, and if a whisper ever comes to my ears of any further collusion between you three girls, I'll personally turn you into the police for breaking and entering into the Corbett's store. As for the rest of you, the same rules apply, and if you tell anyone, you'll be banned from my presence and my home."

With nods of startled heads and sad hearts, everyone turned toward their beds, although very little sleep was attained that short night.

For the first time for as long as they could remember, the triplets lay awake in separate bedrooms at Grandpa and Grandma's house, and with a soft moon lighting the rooms, Della, Josie, and Leah each ruminated on not only the incident of this July day, but on the eye-opening awareness that each cousin revealed during the dispensing of past enterprises of questionable adventures. Saddened and troubled by the evening's divulges and feelings of perfidy, the triplets knew they were embarking on a new stage of life and over a quiet breakfast, a day dawned with them still loving each other but knowing they would now truly take different roads in life.

The triplets continued to see each other at family holidays, get-togethers, funerals, and the big tent revivals held twice a year, followed by dinners on the ground, and though they would always feel like sisters enjoying good food and good laughs, times had changed, and so had they.

The triplets would wed in the order of their birth years. In 1954, Della would be the first of the triplets to marry, and would do so by the age of 18, right out of high school, to a man who was nine years her senior. Meeting at a fundraiser fish fry, her best friend Bonnie's parents were running for the local Rotary Club, and Della and Bonnie were playing hostesses, passing out napkins and forks along with their smiles, when Vaughan Reeves was smitten like he thought he never would be. The day would prove tough for Vaughan, for after five fried fish sandwiches, eight hush puppies, and four beers, Vaughan was about to give up on getting a private moment with the girl he instantly vowed to marry, and the hope that his stomach wouldn't decide to call 'uncle,' sending him to the bathroom and in need of sodium bicarinate.

For Della, the day was fun, filled with many fellows who hoped to escort her home and showed it with big smiles and big tips, but she couldn't help notice the good-looking man with dark curly hair, deep blue eyes, and broad shoulders, who kept coming back for fried fish sandwiches, looking a little green around the gills. But his smile never wavered, and as she took off her sunflower apron, he approached, asking if she would give him the pleasure of her company the following evening for a picture show at the Capital Theater in Charleston. Della softly said yes, with plans made to meet at 6 p.m. under the big marquee. Both went home with a feeling that the future might hold some changes.

The movie, *The Robe*, was a hit with both Della and Vaughan and was a great conversation starter to go with the after-movie dessert and coffee at Winn's Restaurant. That movie and that piece of apple pie led to another date, and another date, until finally, on a Sunday evening in late May in the small office of the preacher of the Westside Church of God, Della and Vaughan repeated vows of love and devotion till death do them part. With only a small suitcase each, they climbed into Vaughan's blue Ford Custom Line and, crossing the eastward West Virginia mountains, spent a week of walks on the beach, dinners of boiled shrimp, evenings of romance, and talks of the future on the sunny shores of South Carolina.

Nobody was surprised by the private wedding, and family turned up as soon as they could, with arms full of gifts and hugs of warm wishes at the two-bedroom apartment Vaughan had rented only a week before the wedding. Settling into a joyful routine, Vaughan began to seriously grow his electrical business, and Della began to grow wider at the waist, for the first of three children had been conceived on their honeymoon.

The months seemed to fly by, and on a cold February day in 1955, a girl named Adrianna arrived with dark blue eyes, light brown hair, a giggly smile, and the ability to win over the hearts of every visitor.

By the age of 18 months, in August of 1956, Adrianna was joined by a sister named Penny with soft green eyes, hair of copper red, and a shiny personality that matched her name, and was a joy to all. Growing out of the apartment, and with the success of Vaughan's business, a three-bedroom brick home was bought on the west side of Charleston and filled with new furniture, a new-fangled television set, and twin beds and ruffled curtains for the girls' room.

Life was sweet and life was good for the Reeves, but life can never be counted on to follow our dreams and plans, and this was proven in the late fall of 1958. Six months into her third pregnancy, with a much hoped-for boy, to round the family out to five, that was not to be. For on a particular day in November, everything changed. Driving home from a doctor's appointment for Penny's check-up on the east of Charleston, on a dark afternoon in a torrential downpour, Della's car was broadsided by a truck carrying a load of stone, sending Della's head slamming against the car window and her body into the steering wheel, and pushing the car 60 ft. before it came to rest on the side of a brick walled building. Bleeding from her head, and semi-unconscious, people rushed to the car, telling her not to move, and reaching through a back window to console a weeping Penny, who survived unscathed but for a few bruises.

In an ambulance on the way to the hospital, Della lost total conscious, and thirty-seven hours later, woke up to a battered body that no longer carried a child. By her side was Vaughan, along with her mother and a doctor, to tell her the wrenching news that she would be alright with no lingering damage, but that the tiny baby boy did not survive. Della's wails of grief could be heard over much of the hospital, and contrary to what was said, Della did suffer damage that bleak November day, not only of a broken heart but of a broken mind, and time would prove that over and over throughout her life.

Over Vaughan's, her family's, and her doctor's concerns, within 11months on a September day in 1959, Della delivered a baby boy who was named Thomas, which she so desperately wanted and whom Della could not let out of her sight or grasp. But family and friends alike had noticed that her personality since the accident was different, and many actions and conversations didn't 'fit' into place in Della's world as before. Her love of the boy 'Tommy' was overwhelming obsessive, while the love of her two daughters seemed to wane, especially for Penny—who now showed signs of an intellectual disability and, as such, along with resentment for surviving the car crash when the other baby didn't—who she seemed to almost hate.

Della herself knew something wasn't right, and in the mirror every day, she saw a different person staring back at her with troubled eyes and a heart of change. This troubled Della, but not knowing what to do, and neither did anyone else, and with three small children to care for, Della marched on as if on a path she couldn't veer from and that she couldn't stop.

The years passed at a bittersweet pace for the Reeves family due to the manic actions of malice and rage among bouts of euphoria that now dominated their lives. One week would be filled with fists that beat Vaughan or the girls, while another week would be blessed with a picnic and fishing or an oceanside vacation of peace and fun. Every day was a day of the unknown, not knowing what it would hold.

Over time, the strain of life with Della would take its toll on Vaughan. In 1973, after too many years of trying to live with the wife he had so deeply loved but no longer knew, and at times actually feared, Vaughan divorced Della. In hopes of protecting his children from further damage, Vaughan tried desperately to obtain custody of Penny and Tommy, but no degree of filing petitions and pleadings before a judge would change the court's decision to remove them from Della. Adrianna, now living on her own, along with her dad, watched the mess from a distance.

The abuse to Penny escalated even more as the years moved on until Penny was 18 years old. With the aid of an uncle and aunt, who many times had tried to rescue Penny, she fled the childhood home filled with cruelty, into a tiny studio apartment and a part-time job of cleaning offices. Though unsure and fearful at being on her own, Penny had found a small peace and, for the first time in her memory, spent the days without dread and nights without nightmares. Both the Jackson and the Reeves families supported Penny in any way they could and rooted for her new freedom, but there were still concerns, and time would prove their uneasiness was real.

In her 20th year, while eating lunch at the Rose City Cafeteria, Penny met a young man who was much like her, and within four months, they were married and expecting a child. In the summer of 1977, Penny delivered healthy fraternal twins, a boy and a girl. Naming them Chad and Lorrie, the family prayed that Penny had finally found stability and clarity, but that was not to be.

Impaired from birth and battered by Della's beating, Penny proved to be unstable and worrisome. Her husband, who faced his own mental and physical challenges, was unable to care for the twins either, and with no family members able to take over their care, by the time the twins were two years old, they were removed from Penny's home and adopted together by a couple with no children. Due to several assorted problems between them, Penny and her husband were divorced. And struggling with daily living, Penny eventually moved to Florida to be near Vaughan, who had relocated there. He assisted her there, along with Adrianna, who would eventually take full responsibilitly for Penny's care and welfare for decades to come. As the years moved on, the twins were occasionally heard from, but Penny showed no interest. Residing in Florida, her scarred and troubled life would be filled with a difficult aging, a greater descent into her lost mind, and the sole comfort of her beloved cats.

The favorite child Tommy's fate was to be as bitter and cruel as Penny's, as far as life was concerned, for the years of being pampered and spoiled had produced outwardly a seemingly pleasant young man to the world, when in reality one who had lived a life with Della's insanity and no father's wisdom to guild him, had grown into a much-troubled and disturbed soul. Tommy was a stunningly handsome child and young man with a bright mind, who could charm men and women alike, but by his mid-twenties, he began to show the same afflictions shared with Penny.

Della could not, or chose not to, accept her beautiful son's slide into a world she did not want for him. Always there to protect, shield, and provide whenever Tommy wanted, his life became one of drinking, drugs, and parties. He never married, and though he had a few serious relationships, his selfish desires kept any woman who loved him at a distance, for life with Tommy was one long run toward the border of insanity.

On a bitter cold late winter afternoon, with plans on his mind, a somewhat intoxicated Tommy left his apartment to attend an event of varing indulgences some of which would be illegal. But Tommy's hopeful objective was not to be, and what was later surmised, Tommy tripped and fell head first onto a concrete curb, and where Thomas Mark Reeves would die almost instantly. Not found for several hours in the fading light of a darkening evening, Tommy died alone and lost in his world of self abuse. Though bereaved by many, it was a shock to all that Della shed no tears at the news, and only seemed to remember, and speak, of the fair-haired child she adored all those years ago.

Della died at the age of 84 years, spending the last five years of her life in a nursing home. Only a few family members came regularly to visit, which she always enjoyed, but whether it was her mild dementia or of her choosing, Della's conversations would only involve certain aspects of her past that were of her childhood and happy times. The years of abuse to her husband and children were never spoken of, as if they had never existed, and Della now lived in a world that had held a different ending on a road less traveled.

Della was buried in the Jackson Cemetery next to her beloved son, Tommy, with daughter Adrianna, two brothers, and a few cousins to mourn her, many pondering with sadness how an event of just one life can result in misery for so many others.

Vaughan lived to the old age of 94 in pleasant surroundings, of which he knew nothing, for Alzheimer's had claimed his mind many years earlier. Vaughan slipped away one night in his sleep to be mourned by Adianna and a confused Penny, who was all that was left from those years of the past.

As for Adrianna, she would marry two times and have two sons. The hauntings from the abuse followed her through life like the contrails of passing jets, always behind her to remind her of those days but fading away to allow happiness to stay close by. Adrianna still rose with the sun every day, with a thankful heart that she suffered none of the struggles that Penny and Tommy had endured, and that life had led her on a different path that allowed her to escape the foils of Della that could have been hers, too.

The second triplet, Josie, would wed at the age of 19 years, becoming the wife of a handsome, blue-eyed, blond-haired man whose sunbeam smile lit up her world the first time they met in 1955 at a revival at the Sunlight Baptist Church on a warm fall evening. Only two years older than her, Raymond Lee Parmley was a simple man with a kind heart and of many talents, repairing or rebuilding about anything that needed repaired, and decided to put those abilities to use for the Columbia Gas Company, maintaining pumper stations over a four-county area, where through the years he would earn awards and the respect of many co-workers but not large salaries. Josie served as a hostess at the Diamond Department Store's upscale Luncheonette in Charleston, West Virginia, where she rubbed elbows with the leading citizens of Kanawha County, where she learned to savor the better possessions in life, and where, over time, she learned to grow disdainful to the trifles that filled her world.

But at the beginning, when their world was beautiful and bright like a new silver dollar, Josie and Raymond Lee weren't bothered by their differences in the life around them and saw what lay ahead as an adventure to be enjoyed each day. The small house they rented before their wedding would fit the bill, for the rent was cheap, and they could save for a place of their own.

So, on a sunny but chilly day in March in 1956, with their parents, Della, Leah, and a few close friends, Josie and Raymond Lee said, "I do," and left for a week of love-making and sunshine on the shores of Myrtle Beach. As they lay in their beachside room, snuggled together, they shared dreams and made plans for what they hoped the future would hold, and upon returning home, they began to build on those premises. In their third year of bliss, Josie became pregnant, and she and Raymond Lee felt that their world would now be complete. They celebrated with a Saturday lunch at the Diamond Luncheonette, where Josie shared her news with co-workers, as Raymond Lee would do at work on Monday. Life moved right along, and all went well, with a baby girl arriving in December of 1959. Chubby, blue-eyed, blond, and curly-haired, baby Deena was the delight of her parents and grandparents.

Returning to work at the Luncheonette with the baby settled in her mother Susanna's care, Josie was happy to be earning money again for the home they were saving to purchase, and also for the good discount on clothing for Deena. But within five months, Josie was pregnant again, much to her dismay, and though excited, she and Raymond Lee were surprised by the soon-to-be new addition, as precautions had been taken. In February of 1960, a delightful baby boy arrived, who was named Sean.

Within a few months, Josie knew she would not be returning to work, but she and Raymond Lee felt all would be fine, with plans still in place and a little tightening of their belts. With two little ones to keep her on her toes, Josie was shocked to discover she was pregnant again!

How could this be? She was on the 'pill,' which had come on the market a year early, and as were many of her family members and friends! Raymond Lee, coming from a big family, was okay with a large family himself, but three within three years was even a bit much for him. Josie and Raymond Lee, though money had been saved, knew there was not enough to buy a house, but also knowing they had to move due to a shortage of space, left the little rental house behind and with everything they owned, including two and a half kids, moved to a larger rental house, which was to be the future pattern for many years and was to be the start of Josie's fall into depression.

In the fall of 1961, another boy arrived. Baby Jared was cute, good-natured, and adored by Deena. Josie, by now, was beginning to struggle under the strain of three babies, and family members, especially her mother, Susanna, were noticing signs that worried them. So, when Josie became pregnant yet again within a few months of Jared's birth, Raymond Lee and others grew even more concerned.

Josie, along with her mother and three children, walked into the doctor's office, demanding to know why birth control wasn't working and wanting answers. Stunned as well as Josie by another pregnancy, he proceeded to say that in some women, the pill simply wasn't strong enough and ovulation and pregnancy continued, of which Josie was one. Sobbing and saying she could not and did not want more children, the doctor said the only solution was a tubal ligation, which could be performed upon the birth of this last baby. That evening with a child on each knee, Raymond Lee just stared while Josie told him of the reason for the failed birth control, and though it made him a little disappointed, he agreed they could not have more children after baby number four.

On a warm day in October of 1962, baby four arrived, matching the other three with blue eyes, blond curly hair, cuddly chubbiness, and a good set of lungs. Bridget did turn out to be the last of the Parmley's children, and it was without regret. And though they loved their four 'little peanuts' dearly, both Josie and Raymond Lee were grateful to get back to dreams and plans. Outgrowing their rental yet again, Josie's mother and step-father, Susanna and Jasper Thompson, dug into their savings and purchased a small house for their only child and her family in the little neighboring town of Big Chimney. It was a perfect fit and in good repair with three bedrooms, two bathrooms, a large yard with pine trees with big branches for swings, space for a garden, and a little shed for Raymond Lee to tinker about in.

As the house took shape and the family settled into a routine, Raymond had to take a second job in the evenings and on Saturday's, at a local tire shop to continue to meet the needs of a family of six, which meant that even with Susanna helping as much as she could, Josie's days were long and arduous. All seemed to be going along smoothly and on keel, but life hardly ever goes as intended, and this would prove to be true for the Parmleys.

In the many years preceding, a time before Raymond Lee appeared, while enjoying the naïve and youthful days with Della and Leah, Josie's mother, Susanna Jackson Lane, began to see flickers of erratic behavior in Franklin Lane, her first husband and the father of Josie. What started as mild complaining or condemnation of her, Franklin slowly changed to eventually become an abusive and wild-eyed man. His consumption of alcohol would contribute even more to his black, manic moods. After many night of fists and vituperative attacks, with Franklin in an alcoholic stupor, Susanna would sneak from her home with a few belongings of hers and six-year-old Josie's, steal away to a neighbor's house till dawn and where her brother, Owen, arrived to take her and Josie to the safety of the Jackson farm.

Franklin, with a hangdog face, would appeal to Susanna many times for forgiveness over the next year, but she stood firm in her decision that held no regrets. Susanna divorced Franklin, and over some years would eventually meet and win the heart of a long-time bachelor, Jasper Thompson, a kind man who not only loved her but her daughter too, and accepted and treated Josie as his own. It was heard that Franklin left West Virginia, while others said he was in & out of a sanitarium, but wherever he was, he walked out of their lives forever. There is a saying that states, "You can walk away from life but something is always left behind", and whatever had affected Franklin Lane's mind remained inescapably behind.

By the time Bridget, the last of the Parmley's children, was three years old, family and friends began to notice changes in Josie, and they weren't always for the best. Though a good mother and one who loved her children, Josie was beginning to fray at the edges. It seemed like no matter how much Raymond Lee worked to fulfill her heart's yearnings, or how much Susanna helped ease her burdens, life for Josie was not what she had always thought it would be. The years of working at the grand Diamond Department Store and wandering through the beautiful store filled with beautiful things had left Josie with a hunger and dreams that could not be fulfilled, and with the manic moods of her father beginning to appear, the mirror of her life began to crack and shatter.

The first sign came when she failed to pick up Deena from school for a dentist appointment, and when she could not be reached, a worried Susanna and Jasper collected Deena, along with Sean and Jared, arriving at the Parmley house, which was empty except for the family dog. Josie's car sat in the driveway, and concerned ever greater, Susanna rang the doorbell of Josie's neighbor, Mrs. Hawkins, where she was told that while tending her flowers earlier, Mrs. Hawkins had waved to Josie and Bridget, as they strolled off to the small path that led to the nearby forest.

It was a 'stroll' that turned out to be four hour long over the hills surrounding the little town of Big Chimney, and when arriving home with an exhausted and teary-eyed child on her shoulder, Josie causally stated, "Bridget and I needed fresh air and it was a beautiful day for a walk."

On a dreary, bitter 28-degree day with her and Bridget cold to the bone, Raymond Lee, along with her parents, stared at her in ponderment, with Raymond Lee saying, "We were all worried sick, Josie. Please, please, don't ever do that again."

This day would serve as the catalyst for a life of angst for Josie and those who loved her.

One event after another would lead the years into turmoil, never knowing what would occur or when, with Susanna watching Josie descend into depths that followed in the footsteps of Josie's father, Franklin. When Josie felt crushed by the weight of marriage, motherhood, and lost dreams, she knew an escape was to be had. With bouts of crazed moods, dissatisfaction, and unhappiness, Josie began to have secret trysts, rendezvous, spending sprees, and disappearances for many days with men she had met over the CB radio.

The first vanishing left Raymond Lee distraught with worry, with feverish searches of her favorite haunts, and so thankful for the help of Susanna and Jasper, who cared for his little family and home. She'd return feeling contrite and asking for forgiveness, which Raymond Lee would always give her. Savage and violent quarrels became a regular event with scenes of knives and guns bandied about, but through all of this, their children never suffered physical abuse and were actually showered with affection and love in a world of chaos. But the sphere of borderline madness that Deena, Sean, Jared, and Bridget lived through would change their lives and carry within it the troubled pictures and voices forever.

One by one, the Parmley offspring left the house they called home, and each in their own way would seek peace. Sean and Jared moved out of state and hundreds of miles away from West Virginia, and though pictures of grandchildren were shared, they maintained very little contact with Josie and Raymond Lee. Deena and Bridget stayed in nearby areas, and though they tried to help their mother, it was a tough road to travel between the 'here & now' and the junctions of passing memories. At this point, Josie and Raymond Lee were in their early 60s, without children at home, with financial pressures relieved, with Josie's struggles somewhat calmed and contained, and with a fragile truce in place, the days of a brief peace were accorded them both.

On a hot day in July of 1996, Raymond Lee said to a co-worker that he didn't feel well and went to sit down on the running board of a gas company truck. Taking a drink of cold water and feeling a bit better, Raymond Lee stood to return to work when his head felt like a sledgehammer had slammed into it, and his body hit the ground with a massive stroke. Loading Raymond Lee into the back seat of a truck, fellow workers drove him to the Charleston General Hospital, where Raymond Lee and the grim reaper fought a battle for his body and mind. In the end, Raymond Lee won, but it came at a cost. Raymond Lee was never to walk again, use the left side of his body well, or speak very coherently, though his mind was still sharp.

Josie took Raymond Lee home a month afterwards. The boys, Sean and Jared, came in to visit briefly and never came again. The girls, Deena and Bridget, came as often as they could, but with lives of their own, it was difficult. And Susanna and Jasper, who had been Josie stalwarts through the years, did as much as they could but age and infirmities had slowed many of their previous efforts. So, Josie once more faced a world that disappointed her and was filled with bitterness, and with a husband filled with resentment at his incapabilities, the truce was gone, and the battlefield between Josie and Raymond Lee was once again littered with broken remnants of the past. After one more argument of cruel words and actions, Josie threatened to kill Raymond Lee, and calling Deena and Bridget, they loaded Raymond Lee into a car, driving him to a nursing home where Raymond Lee would remain till his death.

As for Josie, she remained in the house where she and Raymond Lee had hoped to live a life of joy. But it became her prison where she used alcohol, her CB radio, and her telephone to call family and friends and accuse them of hating her and not helping her, until almost no one would talk to her, except her daughters. On a bleak winter day, while Deena was visiting, Josie seemed to lose hold of the small pieces of sanity that were left of her mind, and in an ambulance, was driven to the psychiatric ward at a local hospital. Josie remained there for many months, where she was diagnosed with a mild form of schizophrenia and bipolar disease, and was treated for both.

Much to the relief and delight of her entire family, Josie returned home a different person, and for several years, rejoined the world and enjoyed a simple and peaceful life that she hadn't known since her youth. But age and time catch up with us all, and as her body began to give out, Josie moved into assisted living where she made friends, played bingo, and thought of the past good days with her mother, children, and Della and Leah. Resting by the window on a rainy March 2011 afternoon and watching gentle drops wash away the dust from the panes, a 75-year-old Josie closed her eyes and left the path of living she once said she wished she could have traversed in contentment and peace on a road less traveled.

Standing with a small gathering in patches of clouds and a pale afternoon sun, Deena and Bridget bid their mother goodbye with unabashed tears of love for a mother who had lived a troubled life of small joys and great sadness. On that day in the little cemetery, Josie Lane Parmley was laid to rest by Raymond Lee Parmley, where both would lie side-by-side in a final and quiet peace for eternity.

The last triplet born and the last one to marry, Leah, chose a man who would break her heart and almost her soul. On a summer break from West Virginia University at the end of her junior year in 1957, Leah caught the eye of a lifeguard at the Rock Lake Pool and Recreation Center in Charleston, West Virginia. At 5' 9," slender, with ash brown hair and green eyes of spring grass, the former high school majorette was a head-turner, and on that day, as she climbed the trapeze to flip into the water, Henry Walker's heart did a flip, too.

Henry, though meticulously doing his life-saving duties, kept an eye on Leah, and when she left for the day, he asked the entrance attendant who she was, and with the said information, he headed home himself with a plan for the future. Henry was a young man of high ambitions and also high self-esteem, and both served him well in life. But hidden from the world lay an arrogance and a need to be in control that would surface and bring disappointment to himself and any woman he loved. As for the present moment, with unrelenting resolve, he would win Leah's heart, and they would build a life he had always envisioned.

As for Leah, she wasn't sure of Henry when he showed up at the door of her parents' home a few days later. In actuality, Leah had much noticed Henry at the pool, but the handsome young man, who stood on her front porch with dark blue eyes, broad shoulders, a sly smile, and the largest bouquet of flowers she had ever seen, made her heart flutter rapidly. Always charming and friendly, he left that evening with a full stomach of the Rowe family's hospitality and a sneaked kiss as Leah walked him to his car.

The start of a whirlwind romance began with those flowers and that kiss and would result in a lovely little backyard wedding under an old mountain magnolia some six weeks later in July of 1957. If only Leah had known what lay ahead, she would have fled that wedding day like the devil himself was chasing, but love in its young days is sweet and beautiful and full of dreams.

After a three-day honeymoon at the Greenbrier Resort in southern West Virginia, filled with blissful delight, both were ready to start their new marital beginning and settled into a furnished studio apartment for the duration of the summer. Henry had led Leah to believe they would move to Morgantown for Leah to finish her senior year at West Virginia University, but unbeknown to her, Henry, a graduate of Shepherd University, had accepted a new job from a large accounting firm in Chicago, IL. and on the day, as she was filling out her forms for WVU, he told her not to bother but to start boxing up the few belongings they had and prepare to move. Totally surprised and confused,

Leah said she did not want to move and wanted to finish her teaching degree, with Henry saying the decision was made, and Leah saying it wasn't.

Henry, flushed with anger, backhanded Leah across the face. Standing as quiet and still as a mouse, Leah rubbed her cheek and, looking at Henry with fresh eyes, knew instantly that the marriage to Henry was a huge mistake and that a life with him would stop this very day. With hooded eyes and a leering smile, Henry walked out of the room, leaving Leah with fear and foreboding. But the pang in her gut that day would soon prove to be more than fear, and as the morning sickness and other signs began to appear, Leah knew she was pregnant, and she knew any plan for fleeing and divorcing Henry was gone.

So, on a hot day in late August, Leah and Henry packed boxes and clothes into the old car Henry inherited from his grandfather, and with hugs and tears from Leah's family, they headed out of Charleston, West Virginia. Henry, with smugness on his face and belting along to a cheery tune on the radio, and Leah, with a heart of fearful bitterness and lips in a silent prayer, rode on as each mile marker on Route 60 carried them farther westward, away from home and family.

After two days of travel and pulling into a Chicago motel at sunset, Leah collapsed on a bed and drew the covers over her, while Henry reviewed a map of the windy city that would claim their lives but that Leah would never call home.

A long seven months later, in the spring of 1958, a baby boy they called Micah, with dark hair and dark eyes, arrived, much to the happiness and love of both Leah and Henry. As much as Henry was unkind and abusive to Leah, he adored Micah and found in himself a gentle fatherhood filled with joy that surprised Leah. As they settled into a life that resembled a family, Leah knew Henry could switch his personality as quickly as people switch socks, so she hid her fears and tears and built a patterned life that would not anger Henry and that would protect Micah.

About 18 months after arriving in Chicago, Leah was allowed to take an evening class, and a few day classes as new friendships were made and the care of Micah became available to her. Though it was what she had envisioned for her continued education, she grabbed at what she could get and clung to her faith in a plan that she knew one day would come to fruition, though how and when lay unknown before her.

That day came two weeks after Micah's 4th birthday, and it came unexpectedly and with grief. Leah's beloved father, Sheldon Rowe, died suddenly of a heart attack on a Monday evening after his favorite supper in his favorite chair as his favorite TV show was about to start. Miriam knew, as soon as she walked into the living room from the kitchen, that her husband of 24 years would breathe no more. Dropping onto a sofa across from the cherished husband of her youth, Miriam wept for her loss of the man she loved and an unknown future.

In shock and grief, Leah began to pack for the trip to West Virginia to help bury her father, knowing that Henry could not accompany her to West Virginia due to a long-planned business trip to San Fransico. But as she tossed two small suitcases and a bag of toys into the new car Henry had bought himself recently, and which she was surprised he let her take, her plan of escape that had lain buried for so long rose to the surface. It took shape in the long hours to Charleston, and it was settled in her mind that she would make it work.

In a plot in the Garden of the Apostles, Miriam and Leah leaned on the arms of Leah's younger brother, Bob, as the casket was lowered into the ground at the Tyler Mountain Memorial Gardens cemetery. The time home with her mother and her brother had been a period of bittersweet respite, but it was a time for Miriam and Bob to hear Leah's unhappy story of her marriage and to share her future plans with them. Leah had hidden much from her family through the years, and as it all poured like a gushing waterfall, her plan was supported by all, though Miriam, who was still in shock, accepted it with tinges of fright, along with a flutter of comfort.

As much as Leah would have loved to have stayed in a beautiful mountain home in West Virgina, she knew several things would make that impossible to do. First, Henry would never allow it and would fight for Micah with a vengeance that could end in tragedy. Second, she had made wonderful friends, as had Micah, and thirdly, she now had classes under her educational belt from the University of Illinois, which, with only another year or so, would see her graduate with a degree that would let her start a new life.

Her brother, Bob, had married and started his own home. After the conversation Miriam, Bob, and Leah had after Sheldon's funeral, Mirian accepted the invite to move to Chicago to live with Leah and to care for Micah while she pursued a degree—not in teaching as she had first thought many years ago, but in the field of psychology for a goal of helping to understand men like Henry and women who are manipulated by them. Putting the sale of Miriam's house under Bob's care, giving away as many belongings as Miriam didn't need or want, spending a tearful afternoon saying goodbye to her beloved siblings, loading her and Miriam's cars to the brim, and saying goodbye to the only life she had ever known, Miriam and Leah left the state of West Virginia in trepidation and faith.

Returning from her father's funeral with her mother, Miriam, in tow, Leah knew it would not sit right with Henry, and she would know later that she was right. Once over the thunderbolt, Henry secretly seethed with anger, knowing that the physical abuse was ended and that his control over Leah and their marriage was greatly weakened. As such, Henry began to think of non-physical abusive ways to punish Leah for her betrayal, and so almost every day, subtle mind games played out in Leah's life. But Henry had to be careful, for he knew Miriam was a fierce woman when it came to her children, and for once, Henry felt a pit of fear in his stomach. Henry decided to play the charm card that had aided his chameleon personality for most of his life, and to be able to stay near Micah, Henry plotted revenge for years.

Leah graduated with honors with a degree in psychology within a year and a half, and to her own elation, was able, after grinding away for two more years, to graduate with a post-degree in the same field of study. It was during the last six months of long days and late nights of weary academic achievement that Leah and Miriam began to plot their escape from Henry Walker. Unknown to Henry, Leah had accepted a position with a prominent counseling firm in a suburb of Chicago, and the winds of change were coming.

Leah rose one Saturday morning, and though with great concern and dread, looked across the kitchen table at Henry and in a firm voice said, "Henry, I believe we both know that this day would come."

Henry stopped still and, with palpable malice, looked at Leah.

She continued, "I will be filing for divorce come Monday. Also, I've accepted a job on the other side of town and will be moving to a new home along with Micah and Mom."

The seasons of calm that had prevailed with Henry for some years seemed to still be there as they stared at each other. Rising slowly, and in a vile whisper, he said, "I don't think so," and with the speed of a cheetah, hit Leah with such force that it sent her backwards to the floor with a bleeding and broken nose.

Getting in a kick that would break three ribs, Leah knew he wasn't done. But Miriam knew he was, and she brought a baseball bat to the back of Henry's head and dropped him to his knees and into total darkness.

As attendants loaded him into an ambulance, handcuffed to a gurney, Henry knew this time he had gone too far, and the consequences would be serious. Henry was arrested on several charges and would be held in a local jail for three months, and Leah would flee for what she hoped would be a new start in life.

With Miriam and Micah in tow, a new job, and a new home acquired, Leah began to really 'breathe,' though there would be ups & downs with Henry till Micah was 18 years old and could make his own decisions concerning Henry. Henry regained some resemblance of a normal life, which included Micah, and Leah found peace for the first time in years.

Micah would grow into an incredible young man, whose loving and stoic support from Leah and Miriam would guide him so well into a gentle and kind manhood. Marrying a girl much like Leah and Miriam, Micah's two children made growing old a beautiful adventure for his mother and grandmother.

Leah was as surprised as everyone, for she swore she was done with men and marriage when life gave her another chance at love. Meeting Gabe, a man who was the exact opposite of Henry and who had to win her over slowly, Leah gave her heart away for a second time, enjoying a tender love she hadn't known before. Ushering into her little world with Gabe, Miriam, Micah, and her two beautiful daughters from this marriage, dinners around the table now contained only love.

At a Jackson family reunion at a shelter nestled under big oak trees at the Kanawha State Forest, surrounded by parents, aunts, uncles, and generations of cousins, and before death had led many from the Jackson clan, Leah sat with Della and Josie where they reminisced about those long-ago days filled with wonderful childhood joys, laughing at the innocence fun and the not-so-innocence pranks that had ensued, and then crossing that thin line between happiness and sadness, they wiped teary eyes from past mistakes, failures, and lost chances that could not be corrected or found. At the end of that hot August day, saying, "See you at the next reunion," the triplets held each other in a circle of tight hugs filled with love and of unknowing goodbye for the last time.

Miriam would pass away, leaving a void that could never be filled, and Leah, with sudden health issues, would make trips to West Virginia fewer and fewer. The succeeding years would move through time as if rushing to catch a train, and would first see the death of Josie, followed within seven months by the death of Della. It was a time of bittersweet memories for Leah, and it caused her heart to move from joyful laughter to gut-wrenching tears. And how she longed to once more hold them in a tender embrace.

Now retired, Leah would move to New Orleans, Louisiana, to join Micah and his family after his career change, and within a year, her two daughters followed suit, bringing her favorite people all together once more for Leah in the grandest way.

It was there on a pleasing summer day on a cobblestone patio under a live-oak tree with the fragrance of a magnolia bush filling the air that Leah sat, sipping a glass of sweet tea, pondering her past and life's choices, wishing like so many before her that if she knew then what she knew now, she too would have taken the road less traveled...

ARCHIE

"There were green infernos and green terrors,
yellow jackets and yellow furies, red torrids and red frenzies."

- James Street

On any given day, Archie Simmons could be guaranteed to be a pistol! And over time and growing into a young man of wild but never harmful intentions, that could be taken literally, as he carried holstered next to a hairy ankle a little 'pea shooter,' which came in handy for whatever occasion might arise in the small country town of Sandy Creek, West Virginia, or the big city town of Charleston, West Virginia—though as of yet, no occurrences had ever needed a gun, for only the ones that involved a verbal threat and a possible 'in-the-face-fist shaking' had taken place.

The sole exception, of course, for firing a weapon was the annual deer hunting season, which Archie and truckloads of cousins and uncles partook of every fall. For that, Archie carried across his shoulder a cherished purchase from Sears & Roebuck that he got as a birthday present a few years previous, a dandy J.C. Higgins Model 50 scope-endowed rifle that could knock a hair off an opossum's backside at 100 yards. But as a child and youth, still under his mother's roof and care, his pistol attitude and the adventures it brought were only of his active imagination with a cap pistol strapped to his side for shoot 'em ups with the backyard chickens. But this changed one summer, when Archie's clever and inventive mind didn't let him down and played out to a greater purpose that involved no gun and that would come to serve many.

In the Jackson family, of which Archie's mother, Ginette Simmons, a widow of many years, was a full-fledged member, and where many cousins, 103 at the last count, were of the first, second, or third ranking in birth order—but it didn't matter where they fell on the family ahnentafel genealogy chart because 'family was family'—and that meant you would be welcome on anyone's doorstep at any time. This was especially true for Archie's second cousin, Charlie Jackson.

Now, Charlie, with his dark-brown wavy hair, dark-brown eyes, and well-defined physique, was a handsome son-of-gun, whose cheery personality and smooth charm were effective assets that made it easy for Charlie to get by with his drinking and womanizing, for Charlie did love his Four Roses whiskey and his 'lovely ladies' as he called them, which were many.

Now, Charlie could never be called a lazy, no-account, for Charlie rose early every day, Monday through Friday, and, not ashamed of getting his hands dirty, did a hard day's work for the town of Charleston, installing water lines for the city water department. Charlie also could never be called unkind or selfish, for his love of family included helping others in any way he could, be it a Saturday of manual labor or financial aid to a down-and-out relative. And Charlie certainly could never be called out for his lack of church attendance for Charlie never missed a Sunday sermon, though many thought that Charlie's personal religious walk was somewhat off the path to the Lord's kingdom, for he was there every Lord's Day with the occasion shout of 'Amen!' as the preacher tossed out threats of fire, hail, and brimstone, and where his slightly off-pitch bass voice could almost vibrate the old popular floors at the Sunlight Baptist Church on Sandy Creek Fork.

But what Charlie could be and often was called out for was his habit of showing up uninvited at some unsuspecting relative's house on any given Friday night, drunker than Cooter Brown. But one disappointing and wayward Friday in August of 1960, when juicy, plump, red-ripe tomatoes and little hot peppers that could make a grown man weep were both ready for picking, Charlie would choose poorly where to bed down for the night and what to eat for breakfast the next day, and as such, Charlie was never to forget his visit to the Simmon's home on a hot evening, leaving Charlie greatly wishing he'd found his way home to roost in his own roost.

At the Blue Moon Tavern on the outskirts of Charleston, with its beckoning of the thirsty from miles away by an almost blindingly lite half-moon sign in neon blue-bird blue, Charlie pulled into a gravel and dusty parking lot, with the cars and trucks of others ready to imbibe of stout bottles and frosted glasses of nature's elixirs. Charlie looked forward to relaxing after a week of work, sitting in a red soft leather booth, snuggled with one of his 'lovely ladies' or playing a few games of snooker with his pool playing friends in the paneled back room with green globed lanterns hanging over green felt-topped tables, but #2 on Charlie's *Friday Night Motivational List* was to partake of that golden-colored Kentucky liquid that warmed Charlie's throat, his gut, and right on, down to his toes.

Charlie always put his best foot forward on these nights with a bathed body, scented with a few light splashes of Old Spice, his pomade brown hair combed in place, a crisp clean shirt showing a little bit of curly brown chest hair, and toe-tapping leather tooled boots shined to a military gleam because he might find himself in the benevolence of one of his 'lovely ladies' for an evening of romance, melting into Charlie's arm while Hank

Williams soulfully sang on the jukebox and inviting him back to her place for a little canoodling. But many Friday nights ended with failed attempts at courtship and Charlie leaving alone and feeling like that lonesome whippoorwill that Hank sang about, and where his tender feelings needed some of his family's consoling.

At about 12:30 p.m., the barkeep vigorously rang the big silver bell mounted on the wall—next to a poorly hand-painted picture of a partially-clad Marilyn Monroe—to alert those dancing, laughing, lining up their pool cues, snuggling in a corner booth, or eating a third bag of pork rinds at the old oak bar that the evening's festivities were coming to a close. As the regulars, and normally a few new-comers, began to gather hats and handbags and pay their bar tab, the revelers began to make their way to their vehicles. Many state and local laws back then about the ills of drinking and driving were none existent or vague at best, so as engines roared to life and headed off to home or the ditch on the side of the road, the patrons of the Blue Moon Tavern drove off, and the flashing white 'OPEN' sign went dark.

Charlie Jackson would start out in his late-model spiffy pickup truck, with the radio calling him to sing along to Patsy Cline or Ferlin Husky and his mind wandering here and there on the lack of a serious love life. On this particular Friday evening, Charlie found himself turning onto the curvy Route 21 state road that led to the town of

Sandy Creek, and turning once again, onto the country road that twisted and followed the Pocatalico River, he would pass by Ginette Simmons' house, where a soft glow from a window caused Charlie to gently swerve his truck into Ginette's front yard.

Climbing gingerly from his truck and staggering slowly up and onto the porch, Charlie heard no sounds but knew that a bed would wait for him in his cousin's dim-lit house. Ginette, who had never been bestowed with the gift of sound sleep, had heard the truck, the footsteps, the screen door squeak open, and the meek tapping at the front door. So had Gabby, the big Rhodesian Ridgeback. And with her #7 birdshot-loaded shotgun pulled out from under her bed, Ginette and Gabby eased their way to the door. Peeking through a knothole that Archie had made for his momma, Ginette viewed a weaving Charlie standing there, and shaking her head in frustration and relief, she opened the door and let Charlie Jackson in.

Charlie mouthed quietly to his cousin as he weaved closer to her, "Hey, Ginette, I think I'm a little tipsy. If you don't mind, can I borrow a bed and a pillow?"

Taking Charlie by the arm, Ginette not-too-gently led Charlie to the bedroom where her sons, 15-year-old Archie and his little brother, Roane, lay asleep.

Throwing a couple of old quilts on the floor, Ginette whispered, "Charlie, plant yourself down on the floor and sleep that pie-eyed bender off."

Lying himself onto the wooden floor, Charlie said, "Goodnight and thank ya, Ginette."

But listening as Ginette left the boys' bedroom and went back to her bed, Charlie rose, and lifting Roane, placed him down on the quilts while Charlie fell into the bed and began snoring almost immediately like a wizened lumberjack. Archie lay awake in the dark, smelling the sour mash whiskey from Charlie's breathing, and grew angry at Roane sleeping on the floor and that Charlie wasn't.

The next day was a beautiful Saturday, with Archie and Roane up early and with an old frayed basket already collecting warm eggs donated by the pretty fat hens that clucked in the yard, and from the garden bowls of big tan potatoes, a bunch of green onions, some red plum tomatoes, and a handful of Ginette's favorite fiery-hot little red peppers.

Summertime Saturdays were special for Archie and Roane because it was the only day of the week that Ginette served a breakfast fit for a king: skillets of ham and sausage, over-easy eggs, fried sliced potatoes with chopped green onions, thick poor-man's gravy, fresh tomatoes that would be eaten like apples, and biscuits the size of a catfish head! It was a morning that the boys looked forward to after a week of watery oatmeal and stale cornflake-filled breakfasts. Food in the Simmons' home was hard to come by, and the weekend tradition of the glorious two-day meals made life a little kinder for Archie and Roane. There would also be wonderful leftover biscuits for Saturday after-dinner snacking, and leftover biscuits to be sliced and fried and served with warm apple butter before Sunday morning church. But today's meal would be shared with Charlie, and Archie knew what that meant—not a single biscuit would be left for an evening treat of sweet milk and bread for him and Roane. And this made Archie grow even angrier.

As Ginette sang about a *'Mansion just over the hill top,'* Charlie delicately walked into the kitchen, looking like a boiled turd, and took a chair at a table covered with a pretty orange and yellow zinnia-print oil table cloth.

Flopping his head onto his folded arms, Ginette said, "Good morning, Charlie," and handed him a large cup of her perfected percolator coffee.

Archie and Roane sat in silence watching Charlie with jaundice eyes and looks that could have killed a patch of pigweed. But an idea had taken hold in the early morning hours of Charlie's snoring, and now that idea was about to be carried out.

The whiff of Ginette's mighty-fine cooking and a cup of strong java had brought Charlie back to a resemblance of life, and now, resting back in an old woven cane chair, Charlie's stomach was eager to partake of those good smells. Ginette served Charlie first because, after all, he was company, and that made Archie angrier still, but inwardly pleased that revenge had been plotted this grand summer day. Because unbeknown to Ginette, while Archie and Roane were out collecting their precious summer weekend food, Archie had 'doctored' some red plum tomatoes just for Charlie, and along with the ham and sausage, brown-edged fried eggs, cooked sliced potatoes, gravy and biscuits, an unsuspecting Charlie had laid four red plum tomatoes stuffed with those fiery-hot little red peppers onto the old blue-willow plate.

After serving her sons and herself, and saying a prayer for all of God's blessings, everyone dug in and scooped up their food in eager thankfulness. The first few bites, Charlie didn't notice much because it takes some slow minutes for the fiery-hot little red peppers to work their wonderous 'eye-watering, throat-burning gasp for air' magic. But when they do, it's a mixture of an electric shock and an attempt at fire-eating!

Charlie dug into that scrumptious meal, with the eagerness of the family dog with a big ham bone, and said nothing for the fried eggs and gravy and other foods, momentary covered what was to follow and what awaited Charlie in the little tomatoes he popped whole in his mouth. For in those four red plum tomatoes were the scraped innards and seeds from those fiery-hot red peppers that Archie had stuffed inside and had kept separate from the other red plums. Archie and Roane ate quietly, watching Charlie while giving each other sideways glances, but no one was prepared for the actions that took place that morning in the Simmon's little country kitchen, certainly not Ginette or Charlie.

The first sign of something going awry was when Charlie jumped straight up and knocked backward the old kitchen chair. He stood still for a few seconds, with the bulging eyes of a startled goat, tears flowing like grave-side mourners, a face contoured like a sour-pickle-sucking toddler, and as red as a garden beet! Charlie grabbed his throat and began to scream like a cat with laryngitis and its tail caught in a door. He wasn't sure what was happening, but for the first time in his life, Charlie thought the Holy Spirit was truly working its way with him, and the angel of death had been sent to carry him to the Hadean world, which he had hoped to skip. But then, through teary eyes and gasping for his breath, he saw Archie and Roane bent over with laughter and pointing to the one tomato left on Charlie's plate, Charlie knew from where his misery and possible destruction were coming.

Charlie, in a fit of anger, suffering, and beaded sweat, threw his waving arms heavenward and yelled out as best as he could, "SWEET JESUS, SAVE ME FROM THESE DEMON TOMATOES

AND THE SONS OF SATAN THAT ARE TRYING TO KILL ME!"

Ginette, startled and stunned, glanced at her mischievous sons and Charlie's plate, becoming somewhat aware of what might be happening, rushed to the refrigerator, and from a pitcher of buttermilk, poured Charlie a glass of cold, thick salvation that smoothed his mouth and throat and earthly soul. Gulping fast and hard, and taking in the left-over plate of hell's food, a shocked Ginette and two snickering boys watched as Charlie Jackson, still holding his throat and breathing heavily, turned without a word, walked out the front door, and climbed into his truck, swearing never to appear at the Simmon's home or any other relatives' house again after an evening of women and drank.

Archie and Roane sat in gleeful wonderment as to what just occurred, until reality set in and the two brothers turned in fear to look at Ginette, knowing that what Charlie experienced this morning—and what might have been deserved—was something their polite and staunch mother would not tolerate.

But to their great relieve, Ginette fully understood her sons' annoyance with cousin Charlie, and telling them with a stern, cocked eyebrow stare, "If you ever do something like that again, a fresh-cut switch from the backyard willow tree will be applied quickly and harshly to your legs." And then to Archie and Roane's wonderful surprise, Ginette plopped down in a chair, threw her head back, and, along with Archie and Roane, laughed until tears rolled down all of their faces. And while eyeing the plate of fiery tomatoes,' Ginette pushed them to the farthest corner of the table, where Archie and Roane looked at those red terrors with a thankful heart, and for the leftovers that were to be savored after all.

When news of the said breakfast event was spread up and down the hollows and valleys surrounding Sandy Creek, and even to the relatives in Charleston, it was good for knee-slapping laughs for months on end. Besides an entertaining and gasping, throat-grabbing mimicked tale, several other things transpired from the fiery-hot little red pepper happening. Charlie Jackson decided it was best to cut back on his Four Rose drinking on Friday nights at the Blue Moon Tavern, which had left him traversing the countryside from lost love, and if not ensconced in one of his 'lovely ladies' arms, to be bedded down in his own quilt-covered cot. And for other wandering family members, upon studying the results of that night, they also thought it best to pass up the Simmons' house of late-night Friday visits and Saturday morning eats in fear of what might await them in an innocent-looking plate of food.

But best of all, for Archie and Roane, they never again shared a bedroom with an inebriated and hungry relative in the little house on the Pocatalico

River Road near Sandy Creek, eating their special Summer Saturday and Sunday morning breakfasts with hearts of thanksgiving. And where, on Saturday nights, sprawled in front of the 20-inch TV that set on a little walnut table, with the black-&-white tales of *The Rifleman, Red Skelton, Maverick, Lassie,* and *The Real McCoy's* flickering across the small screen, were bowls of biscuits and sweet milk, eaten with relish, resting on the grateful knees of young boys, and the deliverance from straying cousins came by way of those fiery-hot red peppers.

Acknowledgment

I would like to acknowledge and give a heartfelt thank you to those who aided in my adventure of storytelling and encouraged me to put pen to paper: Sarah Hudson, Amber Jimerson, Ronnie Melton, Ada Ramos, Linda Reed, Larry Reymann, Arnie Shamblin, John R. Schembra, and Paul Wiseman.

And the terrific folks at Curtis Publishing Company.

You are the best!

Photo by:

 Grin and Barrett Photography

About the Author

It was in the bright sunshine of summer, snowy winter gray days, and the tall shadows of the Appalachian Mountains of West Virginia that the author was born and raised.

The only child of a construction worker father and a homemaker mother in a Christian home where love, laughter, prayers, singing, and extended family was always present, she was nurtured in God's Word with encouragement to let Him be a light unto her path.

Brenda met and married the love of her life, and in the 53 years that have followed, they produced two terrific children, moved to new cities, made wonderful friends, traveled the entire US, and steadfastly remained Christians.

Brenda is now a semi-retired real-estate broker of 35+ years, and a past & present volunteer with senior groups, humane associations, and Meals on Wheels.

Brenda, a longtime resident of Indiana, is where her sweetest enjoyment is with her beloved husband, adored children and grandchildren, a delightful assortment of in-laws, and a handful of little-bit crazy friends.